D1033203

Merry Christmas Quilts

Martingale®
& COMPANY

Merry Christmas Quilts
© 2005 by Martingale & Company

That Patchwork Place® is an imprint
of Martingale & Company®.

Martingale & Company
20205 144th Avenue NE
Woodinville, WA 98072-8478 USA
www.martingale-pub.com

Credits

President: Nancy J. Martin

CEO: Daniel J. Martin

VP and General Manager:
  Tom Wierzbicki

Publisher: Jane Hamada

Editorial Director: Mary V. Green

Managing Editor: Tina Cook

Technical Editor: Cyndi Hershey

Copy Editor: Melissa Bryan

Design Director: Stan Green

Illustrator: Laurel Strand

Cover Designer: Regina Girard

Text Designer: Sandy Freeman

Photographer: Brent Kane

No part of this product may be reproduced in any
form, unless otherwise stated, in which case repro-
duction is limited to the use of the purchaser. The
written instructions, photographs, designs, projects,
and patterns are intended for the personal, non-
commercial use of the retail purchaser and are
under federal copyright laws; they are not to be
reproduced by any electronic, mechanical, or other
means, including informational storage or retrieval
systems, for commercial use. Permission is granted
to photocopy patterns for the personal use of the
retail purchaser.

The information in this book is presented in good
faith, but no warranty is given nor results guaran-
teed. Since Martingale & Company has no control
over choice of materials or procedures, the company assumes no responsibility for the use of this
information.

Printed in China
11 10 09 08 07 06 05   8 7 6 5 4 3 2 1

Library of Congress Cataloging-in-Publication Data
Merry Christmas quilts.
    p. cm.
  ISBN 1-56477-635-2
 1. Patchwork—Patterns. 2. Quilting. 3. Christmas
decorations. I. Martingale & Company.
  TT835.M4795 2005
  746.46'041—dc22
                                    2005003483

Mission Statement

Dedicated to providing
quality products and service
to inspire creativity.

Contents

Introduction

The traditions we create and keep at Christmas are what bring the holiday alive. Draping popcorn garland on pine branches, leaving cookies and milk for Santa, sending cards, and singing carols—within these simple customs we find comfort, cheer, and a feeling of home.

The same is true of the Christmas quilts we make. Setting the scene is an essential part of the Christmas tradition. Quilts lovingly stored during warmer months are unpacked, unwrapped, and put on display to instantly fill a room with the holiday spirit. Year after year, children and adults alike look forward to the burst of color and warmth that Christmas quilts bring.

In *Merry Christmas Quilts,* you'll find projects that not only speak to the traditions of Christmas, but to the traditions of quiltmaking as well. These quilts, chosen for their timeless appeal, are sure to be cherished for generations to come. Look to your stash to create "Christmas Snowflakes" (page 45), which features scrappy-style reds and greens in 18 blocks. Perfect for paper-piecing fans, "World of Christmas Joy" (page 30) is a stunning, high-contrast design that will become an instant heirloom.

No time to stitch a bed quilt? Try the table runner "Family Reunion" (page 37)—just three blocks on point!—or "Crazy Heart Tree Skirt" (page 72), which can be easily transformed into a table topper. Or whip up "Folk-Art Christmas Banner" (page 24) in just a weekend or two and add a little folk-art flair to your festivities.

For quilters, Christmas is never far away. The best holiday quilt patterns from That Patchwork Place books—some long unavailable until now—are waiting for your hands and heart. So gather your fabrics, your rotary cutter, and your holiday spirit, and get ready to celebrate new Christmas traditions as only your family can.

Quiltmaking Basics

In this section you'll find information on tools and supplies, along with instructions for a variety of quiltmaking techniques.

Fabric

For best results, select high-quality, 100%-cotton fabrics. They hold their shape well and are easy to handle. Cotton blends can be more difficult to stitch and press. Sometimes, however, a cotton blend is worth a little extra effort if it is the perfect fabric for your quilt.

Yardage requirements for all the projects in this book are based on 42" of usable fabric after pre-shrinking. Some quilts call for an assortment of scraps. If you have access to scraps, feel free to use them and purchase only those additional fabrics you need to complete the quilt you are making.

Prewash all fabric to test for colorfastness and remove excess dye. Wash dark and light colors separately to avoid dark colors running onto light fabrics. Some fabrics may require several rinses to eliminate excess dyes. Press the fabric before cutting into pieces so that your cuts will be accurate.

Supplies

Marking Tools: Various fabric-marking tools are available that work well for tracing around templates or drawing quilting lines. Use a sharp No. 2 pencil or fine-lead mechanical pencil on light-colored fabrics; use a silver or yellow marking pencil on dark fabrics. Chalk pencils or chalk-wheel markers also make clearly visible marks on fabrics. Be sure to test your marking tool to make sure you can remove its marks easily.

Needles: For machine piecing, a size 70/10 or 80/12 needle works well for most cottons. For hand appliqué, choose a needle that will glide easily through the edges of the appliqué pieces. Size 10 (fine) to size 12 (very fine) needles work well.

Pins: Long, fine "quilter's" pins with glass or plastic heads are easy to handle. Small ½"- to ¾"-long sequin pins work well for appliqué.

Rotary-Cutting Tools: You'll need a rotary cutter, cutting mat, and clear acrylic rulers in a variety of sizes, including 6" x 6", 6" x 24", 12" x 12", and 15" x 15". You'll also need a Bias Square® ruler.

Scissors: Use your best scissors exclusively for cutting fabric. Use an older pair of scissors to cut paper, cardboard, and template plastic. Small 4" scissors are handy for clipping threads.

Seam Ripper: Use this tool to remove stitches from incorrectly sewn seams.

Sewing Machine: To machine piece, you'll need a sewing machine that has a good straight stitch. You'll also need a walking foot or darning foot if you are going to machine quilt.

Template Plastic: Use clear or frosted plastic (available at quilt shops) to make durable, accurate templates.

Thread: Use good-quality, all-purpose cotton thread or cotton-covered polyester thread.

Rotary Cutting

The projects in this book include instructions for quick-and-easy rotary cutting wherever possible. All measurements include standard ¼"-wide seam allowances. For those unfamiliar with rotary cutting, a brief introduction is provided below. For more detailed information, see *The Magic of Quiltmaking* by Margaret Rolfe and Jenny Bowker (Martingale & Company, 2004).

1. Fold the fabric and match selvages, aligning the crosswise and lengthwise grains as much as possible. Place the folded edge closest to you on the cutting mat. Align a square ruler along the folded edge of the fabric; then place a long, straight ruler to the left of the square ruler, just covering the uneven raw edges on the left side of the fabric. Remove the square ruler and cut along the right edge of the long ruler, rolling the rotary cutter away from you. Discard the cut strip. (Reverse this procedure if you are left-handed.)

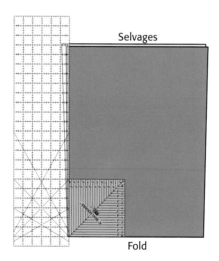

Selvages

Fold

2. To cut strips, align the required measurements on the ruler with the newly cut edge of the fabric. For example, to cut a 2½"-wide strip, place the 2½" ruler mark on the edge of the fabric.

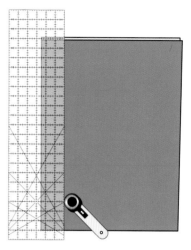

3. To cut squares, cut strips in the required widths. Trim away the selvage ends. Align the required measurement on the ruler with the left edge of a strip and cut a square. Continue cutting squares until you have the number needed.

HALF-SQUARE TRIANGLES

You can make half-square triangles in one of the two following ways.

Method 1

Make half-square triangles by cutting a square in half on the diagonal. The triangle's short sides are on the straight grain of fabric.

1. Cut squares to the finished measurement of the triangle's short sides plus ⅞" for seam allowances.

2. Stack squares and cut once diagonally, corner to corner. Each square yields two triangles.

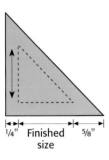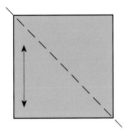

¼"   Finished   ⅝"
        size

¼" + ⅝" = ⅞"

Method 2

This method is helpful when making many half-square-triangle units. Each fabric square set makes two half-square-triangle units.

1. Layer two squares of the same size, right sides together. Draw a diagonal line on the wrong side of the lightest square.

2. Sew a ¼" seam on each side of the drawn line.

3. Cut on the drawn line and press the seams toward the darker fabric.

4. Trim "dog-ears" from the corners.

QUARTER-SQUARE TRIANGLES

Make quarter-square triangles by cutting a square into quarters on the diagonal. The triangle's long side is on the straight grain of fabric.

1. Cut squares to the finished measurement of the triangle's long side plus 1¼" for seam allowances.

2. Stack squares and cut twice diagonally, corner to corner. Each square yields four triangles.

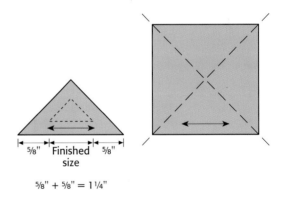

⅝"   Finished   ⅝"
        size

⅝" + ⅝" = 1¼"

Machine Piecing

This section contains tips to help make piecing your quilt as successful and stress-free as possible.

SEWING ACCURATE SEAM ALLOWANCES

For machine piecing, it is important to maintain a consistent ¼"-wide seam allowance. Otherwise, the quilt blocks will not finish at the desired size, which in turn will affect the size of everything else in the quilt, including alternate blocks, sashings, and borders. Measurements listed in this book for all quilt segments include ¼" on each edge for seam allowances.

To ensure accurate seam allowances, establish an exact ¼"-wide seam guide on your machine. Some machines have a special foot that measures exactly ¼" from the center needle position to the edge of the foot. This feature allows you to use the edge of the presser foot to guide the fabric for a perfect ¼"-wide seam allowance. If your machine doesn't have such a foot, create a seam guide by placing the edge of a piece of tape or moleskin ¼" from the needle.

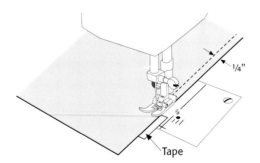

ADDING SQUARES TO RECTANGLES

When adding squares to rectangles to make units with triangle ends, use Sally Schneider's "Folded Corners" method.

1. Place a piece of masking tape on your sewing machine extending straight from the needle toward you. Trim the tape from the feed dogs.

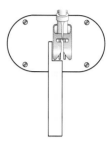

2. With right sides together, position the pieces to be joined and begin stitching exactly in the corner of the top piece. As you stitch, keep the opposite corner directly on the edge of the masking tape so you can sew a straight line.

EASING

If two pieces that will be sewn together differ slightly in size (by less than ⅛"), pin the places where the two pieces should match and in the middle, if necessary, to distribute the excess fabric evenly. Sew the seam with the longer piece on the bottom. The feed dogs will ease the two pieces together.

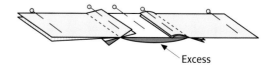

PRESSING

The traditional rule in quiltmaking is to press seams to one side, toward the darker color wherever possible. Press the seam flat from the wrong side first, and then press the seam in the desired direction from the right side. Press carefully to avoid distorting the shapes. Many of the illustrations that accompany project instructions in this book include arrows indicating the proper pressing direction.

When joining two seamed units, plan ahead and press the seam allowances in opposite directions as shown to reduce bulk and make it easier to match seam lines. Where two seams meet, the seam allowances will butt against each other, allowing you to join units with perfectly matched seam intersections.

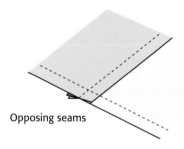

Opposing seams

Basic Appliqué

Instructions are provided here for several popular appliqué methods: needle-turn appliqué, freezer-paper appliqué, and fusible-web appliqué.

MAKING TEMPLATES

Make your appliqué templates from clear plastic, which is more durable and accurate than cardboard. Also, since you can see through the plastic, it is easy to trace the templates accurately.

Place template plastic over each pattern piece and trace with a fine-line permanent marker. Do not add seam allowances. Cut out the templates on the drawn lines. Mark the pattern name and grain-line arrow (if applicable) on the template.

NEEDLE-TURN APPLIQUÉ

1. Using a plastic template, trace the design onto the right side of the appliqué fabric. Use a No. 2 pencil on light fabrics; use a white or yellow pencil on dark fabrics.

2. Cut out the fabric piece, adding a scant ¼"-wide seam allowance all around.

3. Position the appliqué piece on the background fabric; pin or baste in place.

4. Starting on a straight edge, use the tip of your needle to gently turn under the seam allowance, about ½" at a time. Holding the turned seam allowance firmly between the thumb and forefinger of your non-sewing hand, stitch the appliqué to the background using the technique described in "Traditional Appliqué Stitch" on page 10. Use a longer needle, such as a Sharp or a milliner's needle, to help you control the seam allowance and turn it under neatly.

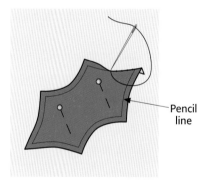

Pencil line

FREEZER-PAPER APPLIQUÉ

In freezer-paper appliqué, a backing of freezer paper is used to stabilize the appliqué piece during the stitching process. Then the backing fabric is cut away and the freezer paper is removed.

1. Trace the appliqué templates in reverse onto the unwaxed side of the freezer paper. Cut on the marked lines.

2. Fuse the freezer-paper templates, shiny side down, to the wrong side of the fabric. Use a dry iron and leave at least ¾" between pieces.

3. Cut around the freezer-paper templates, adding ¼" seam allowances. Clip inner curves, notch outer curves, and trim across outside corners.

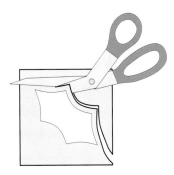

4. Fold the seam allowances over the freezer paper, securing with a glue stick designed for fabric.

5. Place the appliqué on the background fabric and secure in place as described below in "Traditional Appliqué Stitch." Cut away the background fabric from behind the appliqué, leaving a ¼"-wide seam allowance. Remove the freezer paper; spray lightly with water, if necessary, to loosen the bond. Press.

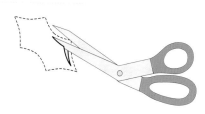

TRADITIONAL APPLIQUÉ STITCH

The traditional appliqué stitch, or blind stitch, is appropriate for sewing all appliqué shapes, including sharp points and curves.

1. Tie a knot in a single strand of thread approximately 18" long.

2. Hide the knot by slipping the needle into the seam allowance from the wrong side of the appliqué piece, bringing it out on the fold line.

3. Work from right to left if you are right-handed, or from left to right if you are left-handed. Start the first stitch by moving the needle straight off the appliqué, and then inserting the needle into the background fabric. Let the needle travel under the background fabric, parallel to the edge of the appliqué, and then bring it up about ⅛" away, along the pattern line.

4. As you bring the needle up, pierce the edge of the appliqué piece, catching only one or two threads of the folded edge.

5. Move the needle straight off the appliqué into the background fabric. Let your needle travel under the background, bringing it up about ⅛" away and again catching the edge of the appliqué.

6. Give the thread a slight tug and continue stitching.

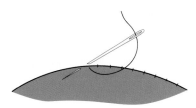

Appliqué stitch

7. To end your stitching, pull the needle through to the wrong side of the fabric. Take two small stitches behind the appliqué piece, making knots by taking your needle through the loops.

8. If desired, trim the background fabric that lies under each appliqué piece. This will reduce bulk and make quilting easier. Simply turn the block over and make a tiny cut in the background fabric. Trim the fabric ¼" from the stitching line, being careful not to cut through the appliquéd piece.

FUSIBLE-WEB APPLIQUÉ

Fusible-web appliqué is a quick method for fastening appliqué shapes to a background fabric. You can leave the raw edges of the appliqué pieces unfinished, or you can cover them with stitching, either by hand or machine. If you're planning to stitch through the edges of the appliqué, be sure to select a lightweight fusible web.

1. For a symmetrical design, place fusible web, paper side up, over the appliqué pattern and trace the design.

   For an asymmetrical design, place the template pattern face down on a light box or over a window, and then trace the reverse image onto the paper side of fusible web. Or, you could trace the printed image onto tracing paper, turn the tracing paper over, and then trace the reverse image onto the paper side of fusible web.

   Trace all pieces to be cut from the same fabric on the same piece of fusible web, leaving about ¼" between shapes. Cut around the group of appliqué pieces.

2. Place the marked fusible web on the wrong side of the appropriate fabric, paper side up. Fuse, following the manufacturer's directions.

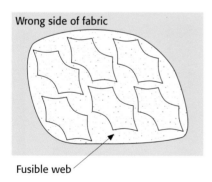

Wrong side of fabric

Fusible web

3. Cut out the pieces on the marked lines. Peel off the paper backing and position the appliqués right side up on the quilt top. Fuse in place, following the manufacturer's directions.

BUTTONHOLE STITCH

Use a buttonhole stitch around the outer edges of an appliqué for a decorative touch, as in "Holiday Berry Baskets" on page 19. The instructions that follow are for a hand-worked buttonhole stitch, but you may also execute the stitch by machine if you prefer.

1. Thread your needle with three strands of 18"-long embroidery floss. Tie a knot at one end.

2. Pull the needle through the fabric at point A, next to the edge of the appliqué. Then insert the needle at point B and pull it through the fabric at point C. Repeat.

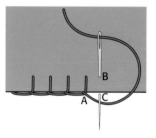

Assembling the Quilt Top

The following instructions tell you how to stitch together the pieces of your quilt top with accuracy.

SQUARING UP BLOCKS

After stitching your individual quilt blocks, take the time to square them up. Use a large square ruler to measure your blocks, making sure they are the desired size plus an extra ¼" on each edge for seam allowances. For example, if you are making 8" blocks, they should all measure 8½" before you sew them together. If your blocks vary slightly in size, trim the larger blocks to match the size of the smallest block. Be sure to trim all four sides; otherwise, your block will be lopsided.

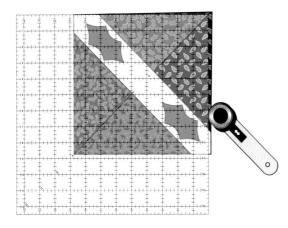

If your blocks are not the required finished size, you'll need to adjust the dimensions of all other quilt components, such as borders and sashing, accordingly.

MAKING STRAIGHT-SET QUILTS

1. Arrange the blocks as shown in the diagram provided with each quilt.

2. Sew blocks together in horizontal rows; press the seams in opposite directions from row to row (unless directed otherwise).

3. Sew the rows together, making sure to match the seams between the blocks.

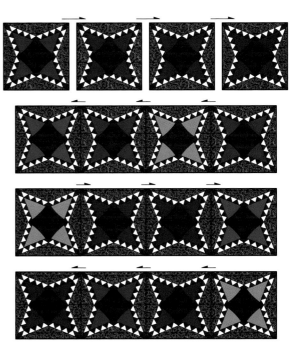

Straight-set quilt

MAKING DIAGONALLY SET QUILTS

1. Arrange the blocks, side triangles, and corner triangles as shown in the diagram provided with each quilt.

2. Sew the blocks together in diagonal rows; press the seams in opposite directions from row to row (unless directed otherwise).

3. Sew the rows together, making sure to match the seams between the blocks. Attach the corner triangles last.

Diagonally set quilt

ADDING BORDERS

For best results, do not cut border strips and sew them directly to the quilt sides without measuring first. The edges of a quilt often measure slightly longer than the distance through the quilt center, due to stretching during construction. Measure the quilt top through the center in both directions to determine how long to cut the border strips. This step ensures that the finished quilt will be as straight and as "square" as possible, without wavy edges.

Plain borders are commonly cut along the crosswise grain and seamed where extra length is needed. Borders cut from the lengthwise grain of fabric require extra yardage, but seaming to achieve the required length is then unnecessary.

Straight-Cut Borders

1. Measure the length of the quilt top through the center. Cut border strips to that measurement, piecing as necessary. Mark the center of the quilt edges and the border strips. Pin the border strips to the sides of the quilt top, matching the center marks and ends and easing as necessary. Sew the border strips in place. Press the seams toward the border.

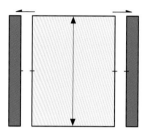

Measure center of quilt, top to bottom. Mark centers.

2. Measure the width of the quilt top through the center, including the side border strips just added. Cut border strips to that measurement, piecing as necessary. Mark the center of the quilt edges and the border strips. Pin the border strips to the top and bottom edges of the quilt top, matching the center marks and ends and easing as necessary; stitch. Press the seams toward the border.

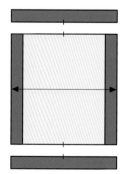

Measure center of quilt, side to side, including borders. Mark centers.

Borders with Mitered Corners

1. First calculate the outside dimensions of your finished quilt, including borders. For example, if your quilt top measures 35½" x 50½" across the center and you want a 5"-wide finished border, your quilt should measure 45" x 60" after the borders are attached. Border strips should be cut to the required measurement, plus at least ½" for seam allowances; it's safer to add 3" to 4" to give yourself some leeway.

   Note: If your quilt has multiple borders, sew the individual strips together and treat the resulting unit as a single border strip.

2. Fold the quilt in half and mark the center of the quilt edges. Fold each border strip in half and mark the center with a pin.

3. Place a pin at each end of the side border strips to mark the length of the quilt top. Repeat with the top and bottom border strips.

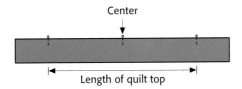

Center

Length of quilt top

4. Pin the border strips to the quilt top, matching the centers. Line up the pins at either end of the strips with the edges of the quilt. Stitch, beginning and ending the stitching ¼" from the raw edges of the quilt top. Repeat with the remaining border strips.

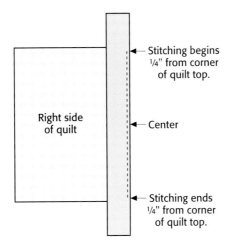

Right side of quilt

Stitching begins ¼" from corner of quilt top.

Center

Stitching ends ¼" from corner of quilt top.

5. Lay the first corner to be mitered on your ironing board. Fold one border strip under at a 45° angle to the other strip. Press and pin.

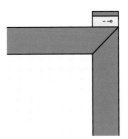

6. Fold the quilt with right sides together, lining up the edges of the border. If necessary, make the line more visible by drawing on the crease with a ruler and pencil. Stitch on the pressed crease, sewing from the corner to the outside edges.

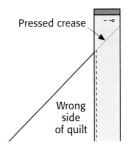

Pressed crease

Wrong side of quilt

7. Press the seam open and trim away excess fabric from the border strips, leaving a ¼"-wide seam allowance.

8. Repeat with the remaining corners.

Quilting Techniques

Hand quilting and machine quilting both have advantages and avid devotees, and the choice is often a matter of personal preference. Here is a brief introduction to the two quilting techniques.

MARKING THE QUILTING LINES

Whether or not to mark the quilting designs depends upon the type of quilting you'll be doing. Marking is not necessary if you plan to quilt in the ditch, outline quilt a uniform distance from seam lines, or free-motion quilt in a random pattern. For more complex quilting designs, mark the quilt top before layering the quilt with batting and backing.

Choose a marking tool that will be clearly visible and test it on fabric scraps to be sure the marks can be removed easily. See "Supplies" on page 5 for options. Masking tape can also be used to mark straight quilting lines. Tape only small sections at a time and remove the tape when you stop quilting at the end of the day; otherwise, the sticky residue may be difficult to remove from the fabric.

LAYERING THE QUILT

The quilt "sandwich" consists of the backing, batting, and quilt top. Cut the quilt backing several inches larger than the quilt top on all sides. For large quilts, it is usually necessary to sew two or three lengths of fabric together to make a backing the required size. Trim away the selvages before piecing the lengths together, and press the backing seams open to make quilting easier.

1
fabric
width

Two lengths of fabric   Partial fabric width
seamed in the center

Batting comes packaged in standard bed sizes, or you can purchase it by the yard. Several weights or thicknesses are available. Thick battings are fine for tied quilts and comforters; a thinner batting is better if you intend to quilt by hand or machine. The batting should measure several inches larger than the quilt top on all sides. Follow these steps to put the whole sandwich together.

1. Spread the backing, wrong side up, on a flat, clean surface. Anchor it with pins or masking tape. Be careful not to stretch the backing out of shape.

2. Spread the batting over the backing, smoothing out any wrinkles.

3. Place the pressed quilt top, right side up, on top of the batting. Smooth out any wrinkles and make sure the edges of the quilt top are parallel to the edges of the backing.

4. Baste with needle and thread, starting in the center and working diagonally out to each corner. Continue basting in a grid of horizontal and vertical lines 6" to 8" apart. Finish by basting around the edges.

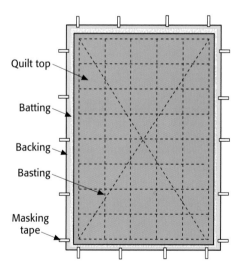

Quilt top

Batting

Backing

Basting

Masking
tape

Note: For machine quilting, you may baste the layers with #2 rustproof safety pins. Place the pins about 6" to 8" apart, away from the area you intend to quilt.

HAND QUILTING

To quilt by hand, you'll need short, sturdy needles (called "Betweens"), quilting thread, and a thimble to fit the middle finger of your sewing hand. Most quilters also use a frame or hoop to support their work. Use the smallest needle you can comfortably handle; the finer the needle, the smaller your stitches will be.

1. Thread your needle with a single strand of quilting thread about 18" long; make a small knot and insert the needle in the top layer of the quilt sandwich, about 1" from the place where you want to start stitching. Pull the needle out at the point where quilting will begin, and gently pull the thread until the knot pops through the fabric and into the batting.

2. Take small, evenly spaced stitches through all three quilt layers.

3. Rock the needle up and down through all layers until you have three or four stitches on the needle. Place your other hand underneath the quilt so that you can feel the needle point with the tip of your finger when you take a stitch.

4. To end a line of quilting, make a small knot close to the last stitch; then backstitch, running the thread a needle's length through the batting. Gently pull the thread until the knot pops into the batting; clip the thread at the quilt's surface.

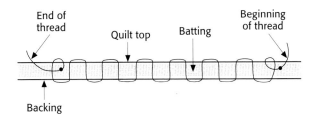

MACHINE QUILTING

Machine quilting is suitable for all types of quilts, from crib quilts to full-sized bed quilts. With machine quilting, you can quickly complete quilts that might otherwise languish on the shelves.

For straight-line quilting, it is extremely helpful to have a walking foot to help feed the quilt layers through the machine without shifting or puckering. Some sewing machines have a built-in walking foot; other machines require a separate attachment.

Walking foot

Quilting in the ditch

Outline quilting

For free-motion quilting, you need a darning foot and the ability to drop or cover the feed dogs on your machine. With this type of quilting, you guide the fabric in the direction of the design instead of turning the fabric under the needle. Use free-motion quilting to outline quilt a pattern in the fabric or to create one of many possible curved designs, such as stippling.

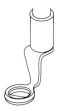

Darning foot

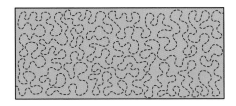

Free-motion quilting

Finishing

After quilting is complete, the addition of binding and a label provide the finishing touches to help prepare your project for years of well-loved use.

BINDING

A common width for binding strips is 2½", but feel free to use any width you prefer. Cut strips across the width of the fabric. You'll need enough strips to go around the perimeter of the quilt, plus 10" for seams and the corners in a mitered fold.

1. Sew strips end to end, right sides together, to make one long piece of binding. Join the strips at right angles and stitch across the corner as shown. Trim excess fabric and press the seams open.

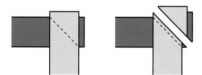

Joining straight-cut strips

2. Fold the long strip in half lengthwise, wrong sides together, and press. Trim one end of the strip at a 45° angle, turn under ¼", and press. Turning the end under at an angle distributes the bulk so you won't have a lump where the two ends of the binding meet.

Fold line

3. Trim the batting and backing even with the quilt top. If you plan to add a hanging sleeve (see page 18), do so now before attaching the binding.

4. Starting on one side of the quilt and using a ¼"-wide seam allowance, stitch the binding to the quilt, keeping the raw edges even with the quilt-top edge. End the stitching ¼" from the corner of the quilt and backstitch. Clip the thread.

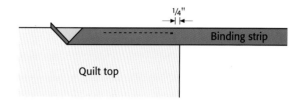

Binding strip

Quilt top

5. Turn the quilt so that you'll be stitching down the next side. Fold the binding up, away from the quilt, and then back down onto itself, parallel with the edge of the quilt top. Begin stitching at the edge, backstitching to secure. Repeat on the remaining edges and corners of the quilt.

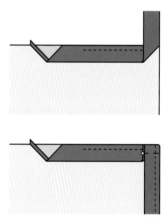

6. When you reach the beginning of the binding, overlap the beginning stitches by about 1" and cut away any excess binding, trimming the end at a 45° angle. Tuck the end of the binding into the fold and finish the seam.

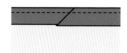

7. Fold the binding over the raw edges of the quilt to the back, with the folded edge covering the row of machine stitching, and blindstitch in place. A miter will form at each corner. Blindstitch the mitered corners.

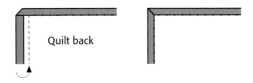

Quilt back

ADDING A HANGING SLEEVE

If you plan to display your finished quilt on the wall, be sure to add a hanging sleeve to hold the rod.

1. Using leftover fabric from the quilt front or a piece of muslin, cut a strip 6" to 8" wide and 1" shorter than the width of the quilt at the upper edge. Fold the end under ½", then under ½" again. Stitch.

2. Fold the fabric strip in half lengthwise, wrong sides together, and baste the raw edges to the upper edge of the quilt back. The upper edge of the sleeve will be secured when the binding is sewn to the quilt.

Baste sleeve to top edge of quilt.

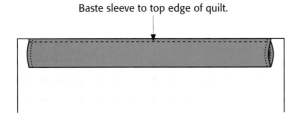

3. Finish the sleeve after the binding has been attached to the quilt, blindstitching the bottom of the sleeve in place. Push the bottom edge of the sleeve up just a bit to provide a little slack so that the hanging rod does not put strain on the quilt.

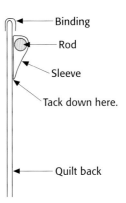

Binding

Rod

Sleeve

Tack down here.

Quilt back

SIGNING YOUR QUILT

Future generations will want to know more than just who made your quilt and when. Labels can be as elaborate or as simple as you desire. You can write, embroider, or use your computer to produce the information. Be sure to include your name, the name of the quilt, your city and state, the date, the name of the recipient if it is a gift, and any other interesting or important information about the quilt.

Holiday Berry Baskets

By Mary Ellen Von Holt, 1996, Marietta, Georgia, 30" x 30".

FINISHED BLOCK SIZE: 8¾" x 8¾"

Materials

Yardage is based on 42"-wide fabric.

- ¾ yard of red print for sawtooth border and binding
- ⅔ yard of cream print for inner border and sawtooth border
- ¼ yard of red solid for baskets and handles
- ¼ yard of muslin for basket backgrounds
- ⅛ yard of gold print for inner sashing strip
- ⅛ yard *total* of assorted green prints for leaves and sashing cornerstones
- ⅛ yard *total* of assorted red prints for holly berry yo-yos
- 1 yard of fabric for backing
- 34" x 34" square of thin batting
- ¼ yard of paper-backed fusible web
- Black embroidery floss

Cutting

All strips are cut across the width of the fabric unless indicated otherwise.

From the red solid, cut:
- 1 strip, 2⅝" x 42"; crosscut into 12 squares, 2⅝" x 2⅝". Cut each square once diagonally to make 24 half-square triangles.
- 2 squares, 6⅛" x 6⅛"; cut each square once diagonally to make 4 half-square triangles
- 4 strips, 1½" x 12½", cut on the bias

From the muslin, cut:
- 1 strip, 2⅝" x 42"; crosscut into 6 squares, 2⅝" x 2⅝". Cut each square once diagonally to make 12 half-square triangles.
- 2 squares, 7⅞" x 7⅞"; cut each square once diagonally to make 4 half-square triangles
- 2 squares, 4⅜" x 4⅜"; cut each square once diagonally to make 4 half-square triangles
- 2 strips, 2¼" x 42"; crosscut into 8 rectangles, 2¼" x 5¾"

From the gold print, cut:
- 2 strips, 1¼" x 42"; crosscut into 4 rectangles, 1¼" x 18"

From the assorted green prints, cut:
- 4 squares, 1¼" x 1¼"

From the cream print, cut:
- 1 strip, 4½" x 42"; crosscut into 2 rectangles, 4½" x 19½"
- 2 strips, 4½" x 27½"
- 4 strips, 2" x 42"; crosscut into 72 squares, 2" x 2"
- 2 squares, 2⅜" x 2⅜"

From the red print, cut:
- 4 strips, 2" x 42"; crosscut into 36 rectangles, 2" x 3½"
- 2 squares, 2⅜" x 2⅜"
- 4 strips, 2½" x 42"

Making the Basket Blocks

1. Join three 2⅝" muslin triangles and four 2⅝" red solid triangles into a strip as shown. Press.

2. Carefully fold over and press ½" of each long edge of a red bias strip, wrong sides together, to make a ½"-wide strip.

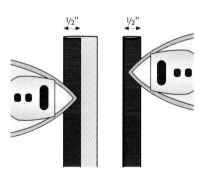

3. Pin the bias strip in a soft curve on a 7⅞" muslin triangle with the ends at least ¾" from the corners. Baste, and then appliqué the basket handle to the muslin.

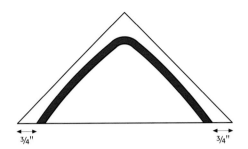

4. Assemble the Basket block as shown. Press.

5. Repeat steps 1–4 to make a total of four Basket blocks. Sew the four Basket blocks together.

Adding Sashing and Borders

1. Sew a gold rectangle to the left and right sides of the quilt top. Press the seam allowances toward the gold.

2. Sew a green square to each end of the two remaining gold rectangles and press the seams toward the gold. Sew the units to the top and bottom of the quilt top and press toward the gold.

3. Sew the 4½" x 19½" cream rectangles to the left and right sides of the quilt top. Press the seam allowances toward the cream. Sew the 4½" x 27½" cream strips to the top and bottom of the quilt top and press toward the cream.

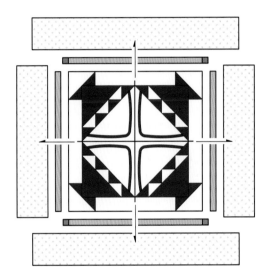

4. For each sawtooth unit, refer to "Adding Squares to Rectangles" on page 8. Sew one 2" cream square to one end of a red print 2" x 3½" rectangle. Trim both layers ¼" away from the seam. Press toward the cream.

5. Place the other 2" cream square on the opposite end of the sawtooth unit. Sew, trim and press as before. Make 36.

Sawtooth unit.
Make 36.

6. Make four strips of nine sawtooth units each. Press the seams open to help these strips lie flat.

7. Sew a sawtooth strip to the left and right sides of the quilt top, orienting the strips so that the red triangles point toward the quilt center.

8. Draw a diagonal line on the wrong side of each 2⅜" cream square. Place one of these squares on top of a 2⅜" red print square, right sides together. Sew ¼" from the drawn line on both sides. Cut on the drawn line. Press the seam toward the red print. Repeat for remaining squares. Make 4.

Make 4.

9. Stitch one unit to each end of the remaining sawtooth strips as shown and press. Add the strips to the top and bottom of the quilt top. Press the seams toward the cream border.

Adding the Appliqués

Refer to "Fusible-Web Appliqué" on page 11 and "Buttonhole Stitch" on page 11 as needed.

HOLLY LEAVES

1. Using the holly leaf pattern on page 23, cut eight holly leaves and eight leaves reversed.

2. Fuse two leaves to each Basket block, and two at each corner of the inner border as shown in the quilt diagram.

3. Use black embroidery floss and a buttonhole stitch to stitch around the edges of the leaves.

HOLLY BERRY YO-YOS

1. Using the holly berry template on page 23, cut 28 circles.

2. Turn a ⅛" hem to the wrong side of each red circle, and use a doubled thread or a quilting thread to make a running stitch close to the fold.

3. Pull the thread to gather, making a small knot to secure. Feed the needle through the fold and out before cutting the thread. This will hide the end of the thread.

4. Flatten each gathered circle with your fingers. After the quilt has been quilted, stitch the yo-yos to the quilt as shown in the project photo.

Make 28.

Finishing

1. Stack the backing, batting, and quilt top and then quilt the layers, referring to "Quilting Techniques" on page 15 as needed.

2. Refer to "Finishing" on page 17 to bind and label your quilt.

Quilt plan

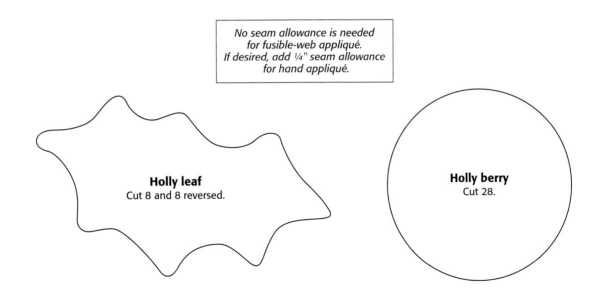

No seam allowance is needed
for fusible-web appliqué.
If desired, add ¼" seam allowance
for hand appliqué.

Holly leaf
Cut 8 and 8 reversed.

Holly berry
Cut 28.

Folk-Art Christmas Banner

By Tonee White, 1995, Irvine, California, 72" x 16".

FINISHED BLOCK SIZE: 9" x 9"

Materials

Yardage is based on 42"-wide fabric.

★ 1 yard of white solid for blocks and borders
★ ¾ yard of red print for outer border and binding
★ ½ yard *total* of gold prints for blocks, stars, and heart
★ ½ yard of green print for vine and leaves
★ ⅛ yard of red solid for bow
★ Scraps of assorted greens for wreath
★ Scraps of assorted reds for bow knot, heart, birds, and dots
★ Scraps of assorted blues for birds and dots
★ 1¼ yards of fabric for backing
★ 80" x 24" piece of batting
★ Optional: ½ yard of paper-backed fusible web

Cutting

All strips are cut across the width of the fabric unless indicated otherwise. Template patterns are on pages 28–29.

From the white solid, cut:

★ 2 strips, 3⅞" x 42"; crosscut into 12 squares, 3⅞" x 3⅞"
★ 6 strips, 2" x 42"
★ 1 strip, 3½" x 42"; crosscut into 6 squares, 3½" x 3½"
★ 5 strips, 2½" x 42"; crosscut 2 of the strips into a total of 7 rectangles, 2½" x 9½"

From the gold prints, cut:

★ 2 strips, 3⅞" x 42"; crosscut into 12 squares, 3⅞" x 3⅞"
★ 2 strips, 2" x 42"
★ 3 stars
★ 1 bird heart

From the red print, cut:
- ★ 7 strips, 2½" x 42"

From the green print, cut:
- ★ 2 bias strips, 1½" x 36"
- ★ 52 of leaf C

From the scraps of assorted greens, cut:
- ★ 35 of leaves A through C in any combination

From the scraps of assorted blues, cut:
- ★ 1 flying bird
- ★ 1 bluebird
- ★ 1 bluebird wing
- ★ 1 bluebird breast
- ★ 1 robin
- ★ 18 dots

From the scraps of assorted reds, cut:
- ★ 1 flying bird
- ★ 1 cardinal
- ★ 1 robin breast
- ★ 1 bird heart
- ★ 2 bow loops
- ★ 1 bow knot
- ★ 2 bow tails
- ★ 15 dots

Piecing the Churn Dash Blocks

1. Draw a diagonal line on the wrong side of each 3⅞" white square. Place one of these squares on top of a 3⅞" gold square, right sides together. Sew ¼" from the drawn line on both sides. Cut on the drawn line. Press the seam toward the gold print. Repeat for remaining squares. Make 24 units.

Make 24.

2. Sew each 2" gold strip to a 2" white strip along the long edges. Press the seam allowance toward the gold fabric. Make two strip sets.

3. Crosscut the sets into a total of 24 segments, 3½" wide.

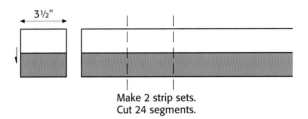

3½"

Make 2 strip sets.
Cut 24 segments.

4. Join four half-square-triangle units, four strip-set segments, and one 3½" white square as shown to complete a Churn Dash block. Press. Make six blocks.

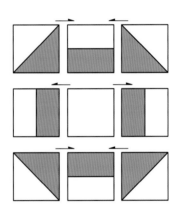

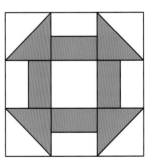

Make 6.

Assembling the Quilt Top

1. Sew the Churn Dash blocks together to form a row, placing white 2½" x 9½" rectangles between each block and at each end. Press the seam allowances toward the rectangles. Piece the remaining 2" white strips into pairs to create two long strips, and trim the lengths to 68½". Sew these strips to the top and bottom of the block row.

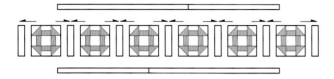

2. Sew three red and three white 2½" strips together along the long edges, alternating the colors. Press the seam allowances toward the red strips. Crosscut the strip unit into 14 segments, 2½" wide.

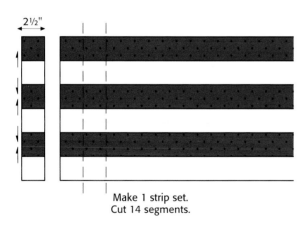

2½"

Make 1 strip set.
Cut 14 segments.

3. Sew a pieced segment to each end of the banner. Press toward the white strips.

4. Join six pieced segments end to end, alternating red and white squares. Press the seam allowances toward the red squares. Sew one strip to the top of the banner. Repeat for the bottom.

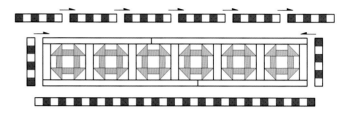

Adding the Appliqués

You'll appliqué through all the layers, quilting at the same time. Refer to "Quilting Techniques" on page 15 for assistance with layering and quilting. Refer to the project photo and the quilt diagram for placement of appliqué motifs.

1. Use the green bias strips to make the vines. Fold each bias strip in half lengthwise, wrong sides together. Using a ¼" seam allowance, stitch along the long edges. The distance from the fold to the stitching line should measure the finished stem width plus one or two threads.

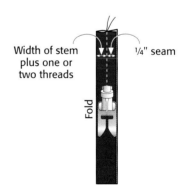

Width of stem plus one or two threads

¼" seam

Fold

2. Trim the seam allowance of the bias strip to ⅛".
   Place the seam on the placement line of the
   vine as shown. Using a sewing machine, stitch
   the stem to the banner as shown.

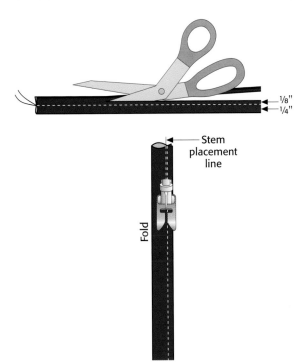

⅛"
¼"

Stem
placement
line

Fold

3. Fold the stem over and appliqué it to the banner, stitching through all layers. This results in a
   ¼"-wide finished stem.

Stem
placement
line

4. Draw a circle 7" in diameter in the center of the
   banner. Arrange the 35 assorted A, B, and C leaf
   shapes in a wreath configuration, overlapping
   the edges and using the drawn circle as a guide.
   Pin the leaves in place and appliqué through all
   layers. Sew a running stitch down the center of
   each leaf to create a vein.

5. Appliqué the birds and bow in place, stitching
   through all layers.

6. Pin the 52 additional leaf C shapes to the vine
   and appliqué through all layers.

7. Pin the stars and dots as desired and appliqué
   through all layers.

Finishing

Refer to "Finishing" on page 17 to bind and label
your quilt.

Quilt plan

Folk-Art Christmas Banner

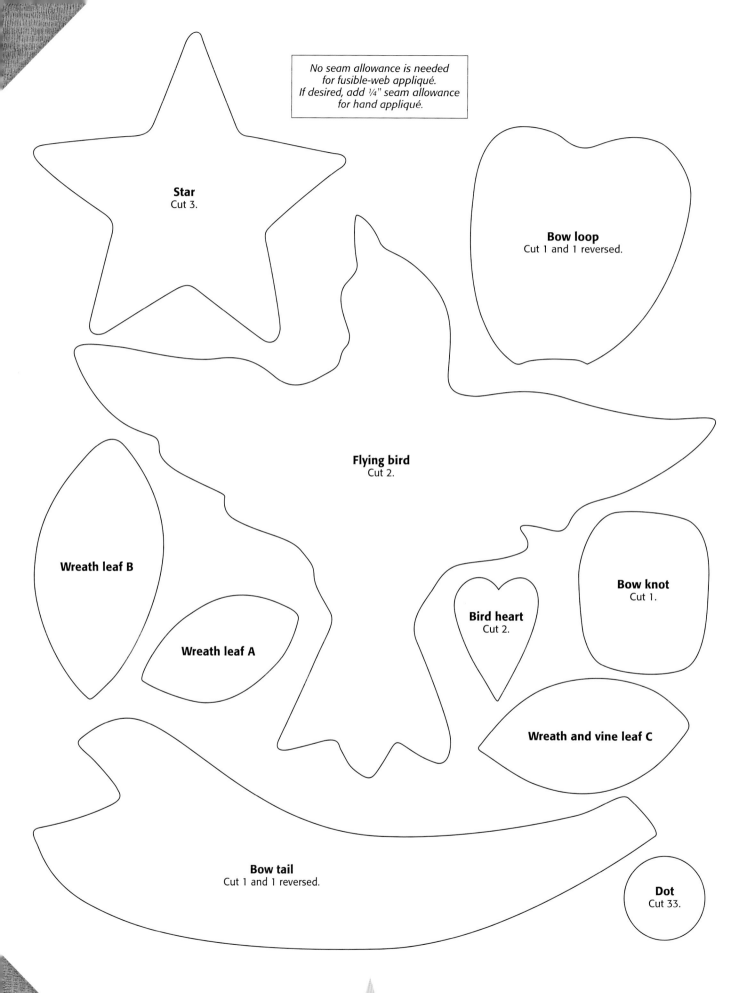

No seam allowance is needed
for fusible-web appliqué.
If desired, add ¼" seam allowance
for hand appliqué.

Star
Cut 3.

Bow loop
Cut 1 and 1 reversed.

Flying bird
Cut 2.

Wreath leaf B

Wreath leaf A

Bird heart
Cut 2.

Bow knot
Cut 1.

Wreath and vine leaf C

Bow tail
Cut 1 and 1 reversed.

Dot
Cut 33.

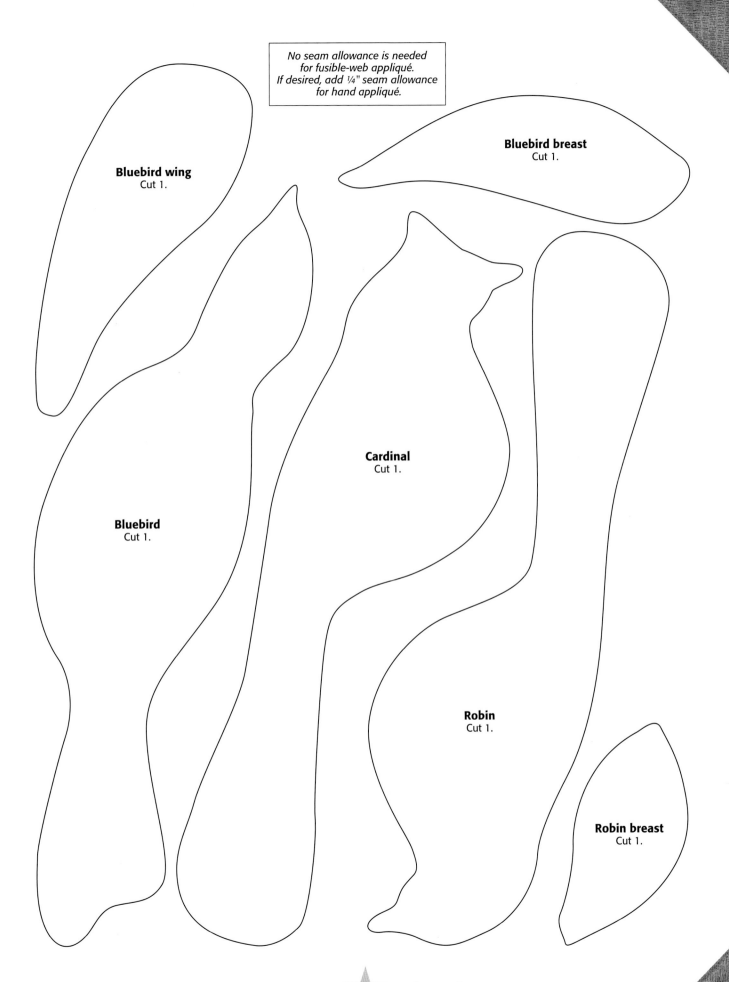

No seam allowance is needed
for fusible-web appliqué.
If desired, add ¼" seam allowance
for hand appliqué.

Bluebird wing
Cut 1.

Bluebird breast
Cut 1.

Cardinal
Cut 1.

Bluebird
Cut 1.

Robin
Cut 1.

Robin breast
Cut 1.

World of Christmas Joy

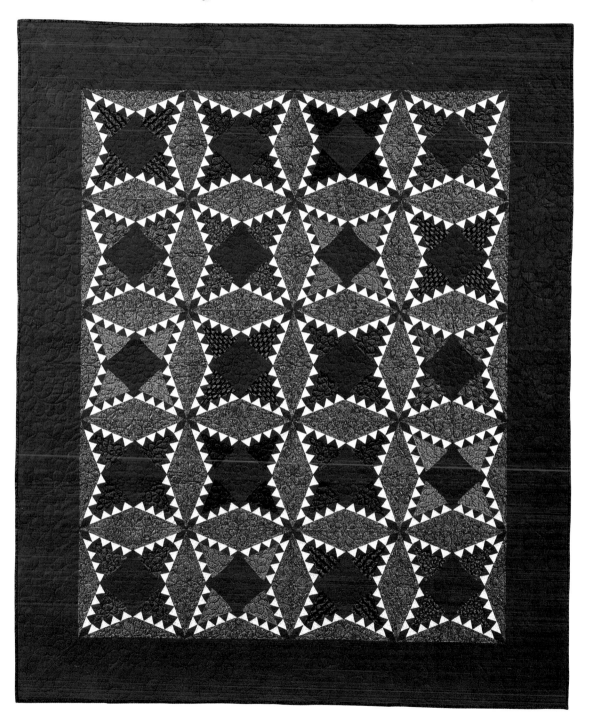

By Beth Kovich, 1999, Woodinville, Washington, 72½" x 86½". Machine quilted by Judy Allen.

FINISHED BLOCK SIZE: 14" x 14"

Materials

Yardage is based on 42"-wide fabric.
- ★ 6 yards of red print for blocks and border
- ★ 3 yards of white tone-on-tone print for small triangles
- ★ 2⅞ yards of red-and-green print for background
- ★ ¼ yard *each* of 10 assorted green prints for large triangles
- ★ ¾ yard of green print for binding
- ★ 5¼ yards of fabric for backing
- ★ 80" x 94" piece of batting
- ★ 160 sheets of lightweight paper or paper designed for foundation piecing

Cutting

All strips are cut across the width of the fabric unless indicated otherwise. Template patterns are on pages 34–36.

From the red print, cut:
- ★ 2 strips, 8½" x 75", from the lengthwise grain
- ★ 2 strips, 8½" x 90", from the lengthwise grain
- ★ 50 strips, 2" x 42", from the crosswise grain
- ★ 20 of template B

From the white tone-on-tone print, cut:
- ★ 52 strips, 2" x 42"

From *each* of the 10 assorted green prints, cut:
- ★ 8 of template A (80 total)

From the red-and-green print, cut:
- ★ 80 of template C

From the green print for binding, cut:
- ★ 8 strips, 2" x 42"

Sewing the Foundations

Make 80 photocopies each of foundation 1 and foundation 2 on page 34. When foundation piecing, keep the following points in mind.

- ★ The unit you place under the presser foot consists of three layers: the paper pattern (with the marked side up) on top and two layers of fabric, right sides together, beneath the paper. Sew on the seam lines marked on the paper. Trim the seam allowance to ¼". Stitch the seams in consecutive order: the seam between fabrics 1 and 2, then the seam between fabrics 2 and 3, and so on until the foundation is complete.

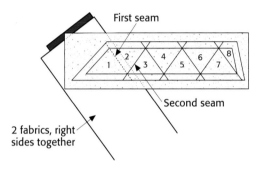

- ★ After you sew a piece and open it, check to make sure the fabric covers its allotted place, with enough extra for the seam allowance on the next seam.

- ★ When the foundation is complete, trim along the outside cutting line.

- ★ Use 15 to 18 stitches per inch to make paper removal easier. If you do make a mistake and need to redo a seam, just put a piece of tape over the perforated seam on the marked side of the paper.

- ★ Do not remove the paper foundation until you are ready to sew the units into blocks. This helps prevent the distortion that can be caused by handling.

- ★ Remember, the finished unit is a mirror image of the foundation.

Making the Teeth Units

Referring to the following directions, make 80 of foundation 1. Use the 2" x 42" white strips in position 1 and the 2" x 42" red strips in position 2, and then alternate white and red.

1. Place fabrics 1 and 2 right sides together. With the marked side of the paper up, place the fabrics beneath position 1, with piece 1 against the paper. Make sure the fabrics are large enough to cover the spaces, including seam allowances.

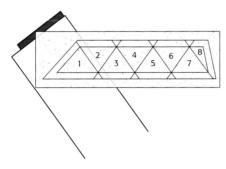

2. Hold the fabrics in position and place the unit under the presser foot, paper side up. Sew along the line between positions 1 and 2, through the paper and both layers of fabric.

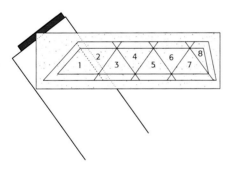

3. Trim the seam allowance to ¼".

4. Fold back piece 2 and press. Trim the excess strips just beyond the foundation.

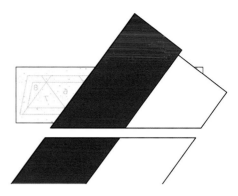

5. Place a strip of fabric for piece 3 right sides together with fabric 2. Make sure the fabric is large enough to cover position 3, including seam allowances.

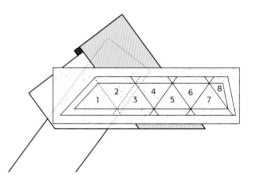

6. Sew along the stitching line. Trim the seam allowance to ¼", fold back, and press. Continue piecing until the unit is complete.

7. Trim along the outside cutting line, but do not remove the foundation paper.

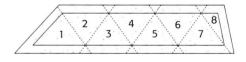

Foundation 1

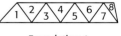

Make 80.

8. Make 80 of foundation 2. Use red strips for position 1 (diamond) and white strips for position 2. Alternate red and white.

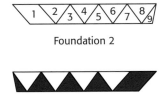

Foundation 2

Make 80.

Assembling the Blocks

1. Arrange two teeth units with a template A triangle and sew them together. Be sure the bases of the white teeth are on the outside edge of the unit. Press.

Make 80.

2. Arrange four units with identical template A triangle fabrics around a template B center piece. Pin the seams, and then sew them together, beginning and ending your stitching ¼" from the end of the seam. Remove the paper foundations.

Begin and end stitching
¼" from edge.

3. Add the red/green template C background pieces. Begin stitching at the ¼" mark, then backstitch, and sew to the outside edge. Repeat on the other edge of the triangle.

Stitch from center mark
to edge.

Stitch from center mark
to edge.

Make 20.

Assembling the Quilt Top and Finishing

1. Arrange the blocks into five rows of four blocks each. Sew the blocks into horizontal rows. Press. Join the rows. Press.

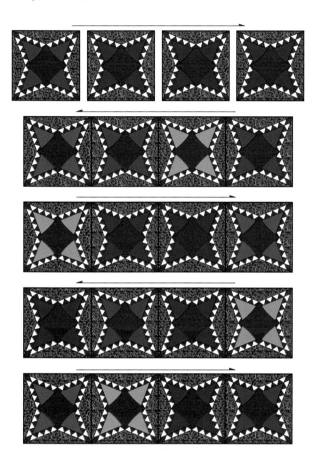

2. Refer to "Borders with Mitered Corners" on page 14 to sew the border strips to the quilt top, mitering the corners.

3. Stack the backing, batting, and quilt top and then quilt the layers, referring to "Quilting Techniques" on page 15 as needed.

4. Refer to "Finishing" on page 17 to bind and label your quilt.

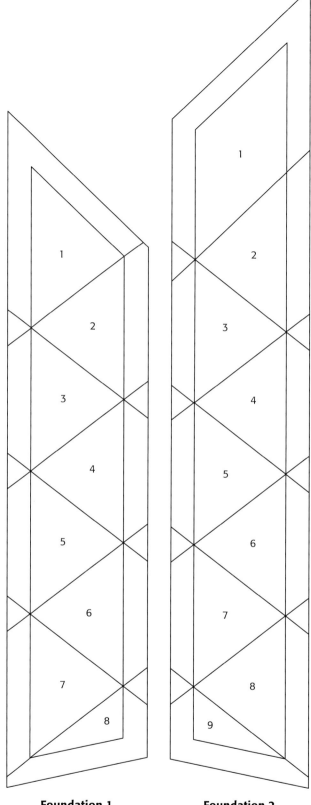

Foundation 1　　　**Foundation 2**

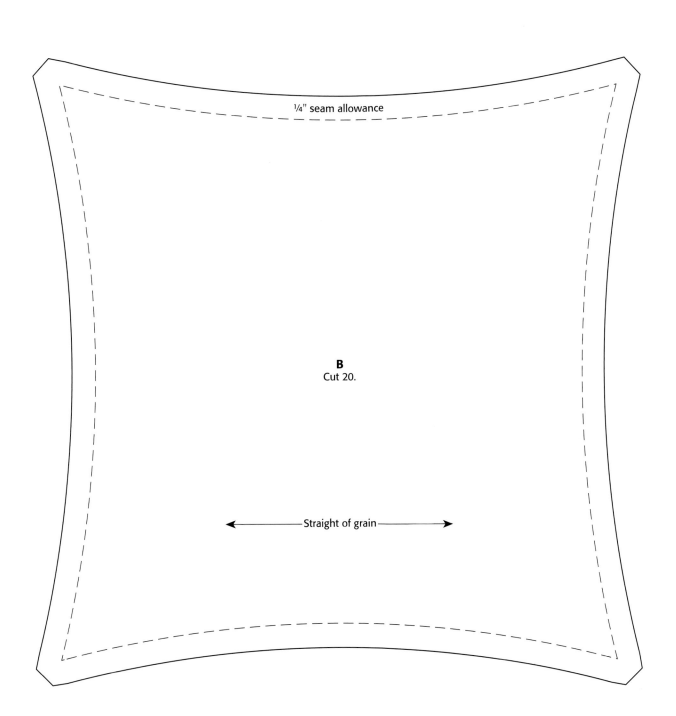

¼" seam allowance

B
Cut 20.

← Straight of grain →

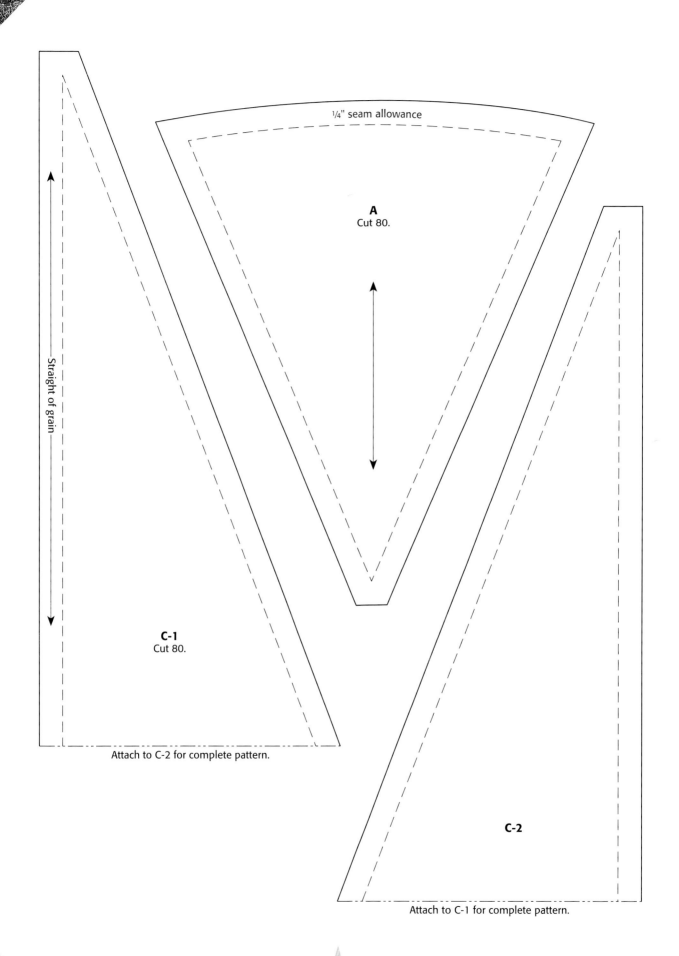

¼" seam allowance

A
Cut 80.

Straight of grain

C-1
Cut 80.

Attach to C-2 for complete pattern.

C-2

Attach to C-1 for complete pattern.

Family Reunion

Mary Green, 1999, Monroe, Washington, 18⅞" x 55".

FINISHED BLOCK SIZE: 12" x 12"

Materials

Yardage is based on 42"-wide fabric.

- ★ 1 yard of white print for blocks and side and corner triangles
- ★ ⅝ yard of red print for blocks
- ★ ½ yard of dark green print for blocks and binding
- ★ 1¾ yards of fabric for backing
- ★ 25" x 61" piece of batting

Cutting

All strips are cut across the width of the fabric unless indicated otherwise.

From the white print, cut:

- ★ 2 strips, 3" x 42"; crosscut into 24 squares, 3" x 3"
- ★ 1 strip, 3¾" x 24"; crosscut into 6 squares, 3¾" x 3¾". Cut each square once diagonally to make 12 half-square triangles.
- ★ 1 strip, 2½" x 42"; crosscut into 12 squares, 2½" x 2½"
- ★ 1 square, 19⅝" x 19⅝"; cut twice diagonally to make 4 quarter-square triangles
- ★ 2 squares, 10⅛" x 10⅛"; cut each square once diagonally to make 4 half-square triangles

From the red print, cut:

- ★ 2 strips, 3" x 42"; crosscut into 24 squares, 3" x 3"
- ★ 4 strips, 1" x 42"; crosscut into 6 rectangles, 1" x 12½", and 6 rectangles, 1" x 13½"
- ★ 3 squares, 4½" x 4½"

From the dark green print, cut:

- ★ 1 strip, 4⅞" x 42"; crosscut into 6 squares, 4⅞" x 4⅞". Cut each square once diagonally to make 12 half-square triangles.
- ★ 4 strips, 2" x 42"

Assembling the Blocks

1. Draw a diagonal line on the wrong side of each 3" white square. Place a white square on top of a red square, right sides together. Sew ¼" from the drawn line on both sides. Cut on the drawn line. Press the seam toward the red triangle. Make 48.

Make 48.

2. Trim the square to 2½" x 2½". Place a square ruler's diagonal line on the diagonal seam line and trim evenly from all four sides.

Note: Sewing together triangles that are larger than needed and then trimming to the required size after stitching results in more accurately sized units.

3. Follow the diagram to piece a Union Square block as shown. Make three.

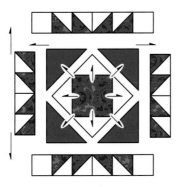

Union Square.
Make 3.

4. Sew a 1" x 12½" red rectangle to the left and right sides of each block. Press. Sew a 1" x 13½" red rectangle to the top and bottom of each block. Press.

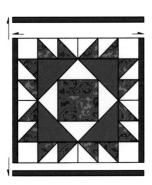

Assembling the Quilt Top and Finishing

1. Arrange the blocks and the 19⅝" side triangles and 10⅛" corner triangles in diagonal rows as shown. Sew the blocks and side triangles into rows. Join the rows, adding the corner triangles last. Press.

2. Stack the backing, batting, and quilt top and then quilt the layers, referring to "Quilting Techniques" on page 15 as needed.

3. Refer to "Finishing" on page 17 to bind and label your quilt.

North Wind

By Tricia Lund, 2000, Seattle, Washington, 44½" x 56½". Hand quilted by Hazel Montague.

FINISHED BLOCK SIZE: 6" x 6"

Materials

Yardage is based on 42"-wide fabric.
- ★ 2¾ yards of assorted light prints and plaids for blocks
- ★ 2¾ yards of assorted dark prints and plaids for blocks
- ★ 1⅝ yards of black print for border
- ★ ½ yard of fabric for binding
- ★ 3 yards of fabric for backing
- ★ 52" x 64" piece of batting
- ★ 48 sheets of lightweight paper or paper designed for foundation piecing

Cutting

All strips are cut across the width of the fabric unless indicated otherwise.

From the assorted light prints and plaids, cut:
- ★ 3 strips, 4⅞" x 42"; crosscut into 24 squares, 4⅞" x 4⅞". Cut each square once diagonally to make 48 half-square triangles.
- ★ 21 strips, 3" x 42"

From the assorted dark prints and plaids, cut:
- ★ 3 strips, 4⅞" x 42"; crosscut into 24 squares, 4⅞" x 4⅞". Cut each square once diagonally to make 48 half-square triangles.
- ★ 21 strips, 3" x 42"

From the black print, cut:
- ★ 4 strips, 4½" x length of fabric

From the binding fabric, cut:
- ★ 6 strips, 2" x 42"

Assembling the Blocks

For general foundation-piecing guidelines, refer to "Sewing the Foundations" on page 31 within the project instructions for "World of Christmas Joy."

Make 48 copies of both of the foundation patterns on page 44. Cut the units apart ⅛" to ¼" outside the cutting line.

1. Place a 3" light strip and a 3" dark strip right sides together. With the marked side of the foundation pattern up, place the fabrics beneath position 1, with the dark fabric against the paper and the edges of the strips extending ¼" into position 2.

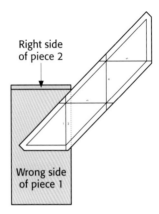

2. Hold the fabrics in position and place the unit under the presser foot, paper side up. Sew along the line between positions 1 and 2 through the paper and both layers of fabric.

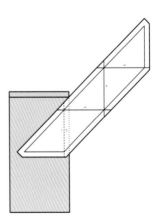

3. Trim the excess from the strips just beyond the foundation edge. Fold back the light fabric over position 2 and press.

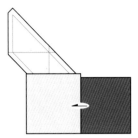

4. Place a 3" dark strip right sides together over the fabrics in positions 1 and 2. Sew along the line between positions 2 and 3. Trim the excess from the strip and trim seam allowances to ¼". Fold the piece back and press.

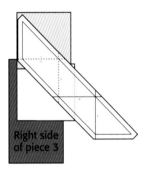

Stitch.

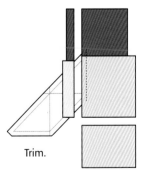

Trim.

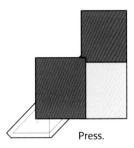

Press.

5. Continue to add strips of fabric, alternating light and dark strips. Trim and press after adding each fabric. When the foundation is complete, trim along the outside cutting line. Construct 48 foundation-pieced units that begin and end with dark fabric.

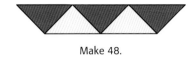

Make 48.

6. Construct 48 foundation-pieced units that begin and end with light fabric.

Make 48.

7. Join a dark triangle to a dark foundation-pieced unit as shown. Press toward the dark triangle. Repeat for all 48 units. Join a light triangle to a light foundation-pieced unit. Press toward the light triangle. Repeat for all 48 units.

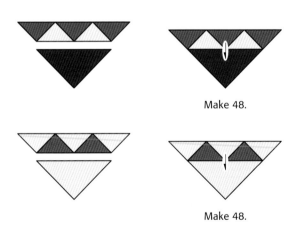

Make 48.

Make 48.

8. Join a light unit and a dark unit as shown to make a block. Press. Make 48.

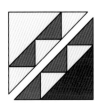

Assembling the Quilt Top and Finishing

1. Arrange the blocks into eight rows of six blocks each. Sew the blocks into horizontal rows. Join the rows. Press.

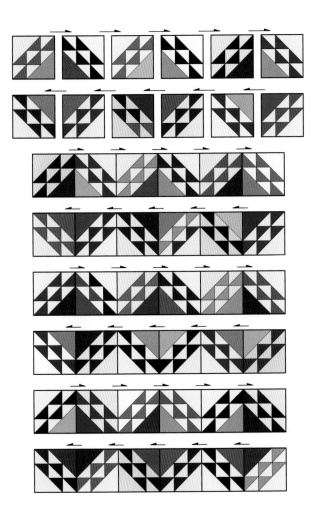

2. Referring to "Straight-Cut Borders" on page 13, measure, trim, and sew the border strips to the sides of the quilt top first, and then to the top and bottom edges.

3. Stack the backing, batting, and quilt top and then quilt the layers, referring to "Quilting Techniques" on page 15 as needed.

4. Refer to "Finishing" on page 17 to bind and label your quilt.

Quilt plan

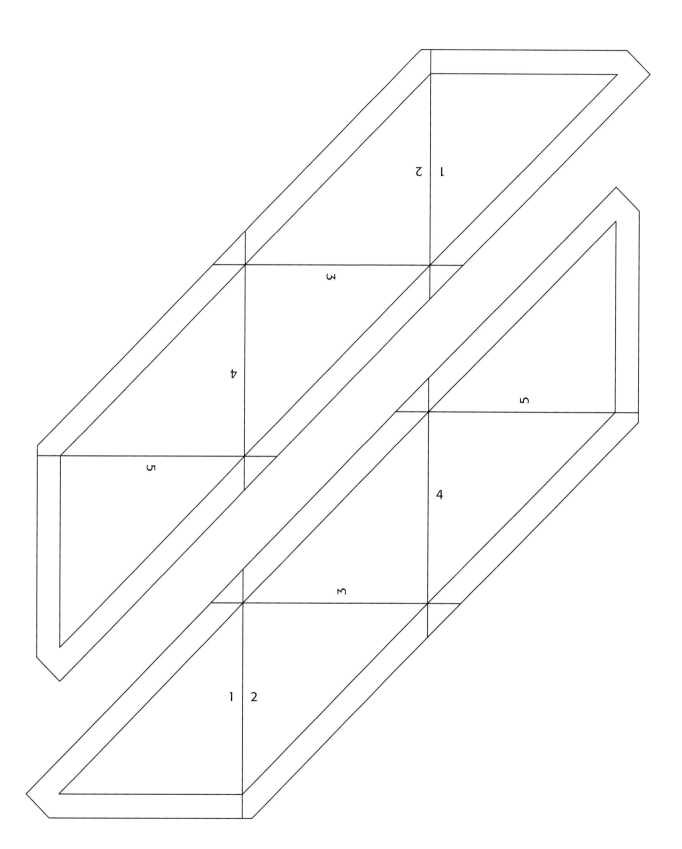

Christmas Snowflakes

By Roxanne Carter, 2000, Mukilteo, Washington, 53" x 70".

FINISHED SIZE OF SISTER'S CHOICE BLOCK: 8¾" x 8¾"
FINISHED SIZE OF ALTERNATE BLOCK: 8¾" x 8¾"

Materials

Yardage is based on 42"-wide fabric.

- ★ 2¼ yards of white print for alternate blocks and border
- ★ 1¾ yards total of assorted print fabrics for Sister's Choice blocks
- ★ 1¾ yards of green print for alternate blocks, border, and binding
- ★ 1¼ yards of background fabric for Sister's Choice blocks
- ★ 3¾ yards of fabric for backing
- ★ 61" x 78" piece of batting

Cutting

All strips are cut across the width of the fabric unless indicated otherwise.

From the background fabric, cut:

- ★ 6 strips, 2⅝" x 42"; crosscut into 72 squares, 2⅝" x 2⅝"
- ★ 9 strips, 2¼" x 42"; crosscut into 144 squares, 2¼" x 2¼"

For each Sister's Choice block, cut from 1 print fabric:

- ★ 4 squares, 2⅝" x 2⅝"
- ★ 9 squares, 2¼" x 2¼"

Note: Cut pieces for 18 blocks.

From the green print, cut:

- ★ 3 strips, 10" x 42"; crosscut into 12 squares, 10" x 10". Cut each square twice diagonally to make 48 quarter-square triangles.
- ★ 7 strips, 2½" x 42"

From the white print, cut:

- ★ 3 strips, 10" x 42"; crosscut into 9 squares, 10" x 10". Cut each square twice diagonally to make 36 quarter-square triangles.
- ★ 5 strips, 4⅞" x 42"; crosscut into 10 segments, 4⅞" x 18¾"
- ★ 1 strip, 9¾" x 42"; crosscut into 2 squares, 9¾" x 9¾". Cut each square once diagonally to make 4 half-square triangles.

Assembling the Blocks

For this quilt you'll make 18 Sister's Choice blocks and 17 alternate blocks.

SISTER'S CHOICE BLOCK

1. Draw a diagonal line on the wrong side of each 2⅝" background square. Place one of these squares on top of a 2⅝" print square, right sides together. Sew ¼" from the drawn line on both sides. Cut on the drawn line. Press the seam toward the print. Repeat for remaining squares. Make 8.

Make 8.

2. Join a half-square-triangle unit from step 1 to a 2¼" background square. Press the seam toward the background fabric.

Make 4.

3. Join a half-square-triangle unit from step 1 to a 2¼" print square. Press toward the print fabric.

Make 4.

4. Join the units from steps 2 and 3 to make the corner unit (unit A) for the Sister's Choice block. Press.

Unit A.
Make 4.

5. Join a 2¼" background square and a 2¼" print square. Press toward the print square to make unit B.

Unit B.
Make 4.

6. Join four of unit A, four of unit B, and a 2¼" print square to make a Sister's Choice block.

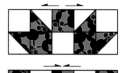

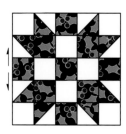

Make 18.

ALTERNATE BLOCK

Join two green print quarter-square triangles and two white print quarter-square triangles as shown to make an alternate block.

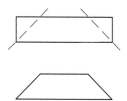

Make 17.

BORDER UNITS

1. Cut the ends of the 4⅞" x 18¾" white print border segments at 45° angles to make trapezoid pieces.

2. Join green print quarter-square triangles between trapezoid border segments.

3. Join three trapezoids and four triangles for the side border strips and two trapezoids and three triangles for the top and bottom border strips.

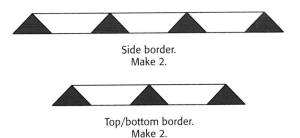

Side border.
Make 2.

Top/bottom border.
Make 2.

Assembling the Quilt Top and Finishing

1. Arrange the blocks into seven rows of five blocks each, alternating the Sister's Choice blocks and the alternate blocks. Take care to orient the alternate blocks correctly. Sew the blocks together into horizontal rows. Press the seams toward the alternate blocks.

2. Join the rows. Sew the side border strips to the quilt top, aligning seam lines; then sew the top and bottom border strips to the quilt top. Sew the white print half-square triangles to the corners of the quilt top. Press.

3. Stack the backing, batting, and quilt top and then quilt the layers, referring to "Quilting Techniques" on page 15 as needed.

4. Refer to "Finishing" on page 17 to bind and label your quilt.

Holly Scrap Quilt

By Deborah J. Moffett-Hall, 1991, Hatfield, Pennsylvania, 86" x 102".

FINISHED BLOCK SIZE: 8" x 8"

Materials

Yardage is based on 42"-wide fabric.

* 3 yards of green print for holly leaves, outer border, and binding
* 3 yards of red solid for middle border
* 2½ yards of white-on-white print for sashing and inner border
* ¼ yard *each* of 8 assorted red prints for blocks
* ¼ yard *each* of 8 assorted green prints for blocks
* 8 yards of fabric for backing (3 widths pieced horizontally)
* 94" x 110" piece of batting
* 49 flat red buttons, ¾" in diameter (optional)

Cutting

All strips are cut across the width of the fabric unless indicated otherwise. Template patterns are on page 52.

From *each* of the 16 assorted red and green prints, cut:

* 5 squares, 7¹³⁄₁₆" x 7¹³⁄₁₆" (80 total); cut each square twice diagonally to make 320 quarter-square triangles. You should have 160 red triangles and 160 green triangles.

From the white-on-white print, cut:

* 14 strips, 2½" x 90". Use 12 strips and the sashing template to cut a total of 80 sashing pieces. The remaining 2 strips will be used for the inner side border.
* 2 strips, 2½" x 74"

From the red solid, cut:

* 2 strips, 4" x 96", from the lengthwise grain
* 2 strips, 4" x 80", from the lengthwise grain

From the green print for outer border, cut:

* 2 strips, 6" x 108", from the lengthwise grain
* 2 strips, 6" x 90", from the lengthwise grain

From the remaining green print, cut:

* 16 strips, 2½" x width of fabric
* 160 holly leaves

Assembling the Blocks

1. Sew green and red quarter-square triangles together as shown. Make sure the green triangle is on the left and the red triangle is on the right. Press toward the green triangle. Make 160.

Make 160.

2. Sew a red/green unit to opposite sides of each sashing piece to make 80 blocks. Press the seams toward the red/green units.

Make 80.

3. Refer to "Basic Appliqué" on page 9 to appliqué leaves to the sashing.

Assembling the Quilt Top and Finishing

1. Arrange the blocks into 10 rows of eight blocks each, rotating each block as shown below.

2. Sew the blocks into horizontal rows. Press the seams in opposite directions from row to row. Join the rows, making sure to match the seams between the blocks.

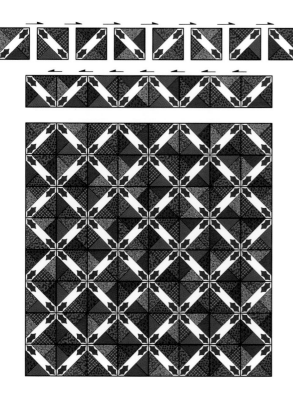

3. Mark the centers of all border strips by folding each strip in half lengthwise and pressing lightly.

4. Sew the strips for the inner, middle, and outer borders together as shown, matching the centers.

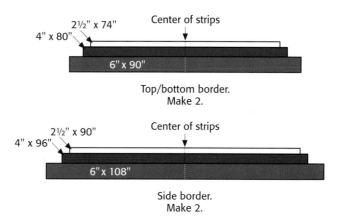

Top/bottom border.
Make 2.

Side border.
Make 2.

5. Add the borders to the quilt top, following the directions in "Borders with Mitered Corners" on page 14.

6. Stack the backing, batting, and quilt top and then quilt the layers, referring to "Quilting Techniques" on page 15 as needed.

7. Refer to "Finishing" on page 17 to bind and label your quilt.

8. If desired, add a red button in the center of each set of holly leaves.

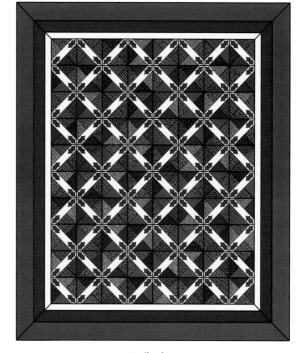

Quilt plan

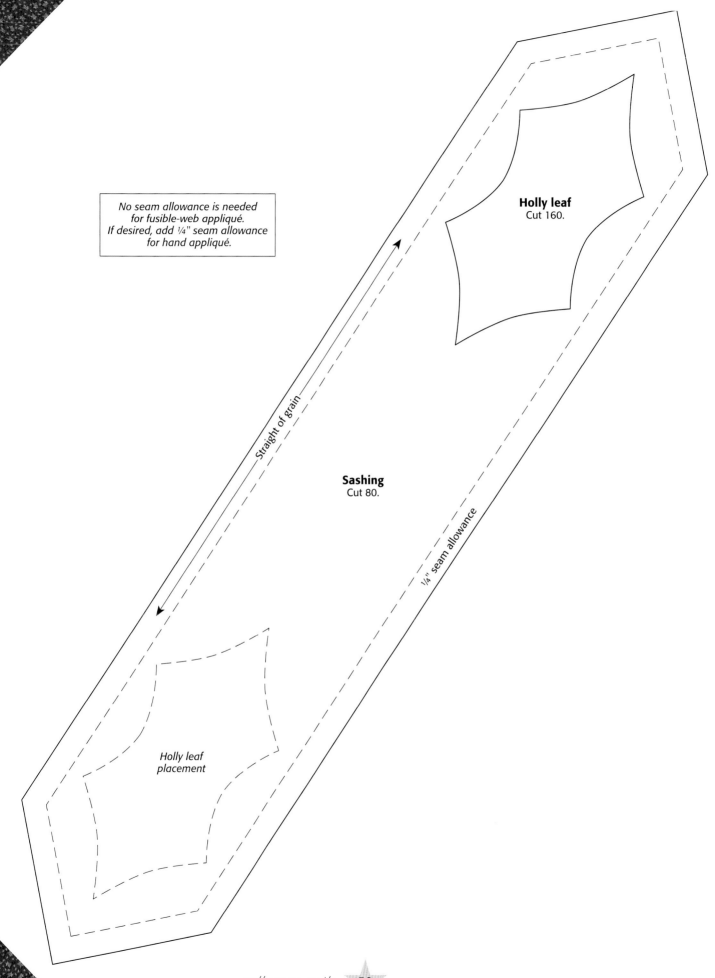

No seam allowance is needed
for fusible-web appliqué.
If desired, add ¼" seam allowance
for hand appliqué.

Holly leaf
Cut 160.

Straight of grain

Sashing
Cut 80.

¼" seam allowance

*Holly leaf
placement*

Cardinal Feathered Star

By Deborah J. Moffett-Hall, 1993, Hatfield, Pennsylvania, 29" x 29".

Materials

Yardage is based on 42"-wide fabric.

- ⅞ yard of floral print for borders
- ¾ yard of tan print for background
- ½ yard of red print for cardinal, blocks, and binding
- ¼ yard of green print 2 for blocks and leaves
- ⅛ yard of green print 1 for blocks and leaves
- ⅛ yard of green print 3 for leaves
- ⅛ yard of dark red print for blocks
- 1⅛ yards of fabric for backing
- 35" x 35" piece of batting
- Optional: Embroidery floss
- Optional: 1 yard paper-backed fusible web

Cutting

All strips are cut across the width of the fabric unless indicated otherwise. Template patterns are on pages 58–59.

From the tan print, cut:

- 2 strips, 2⅜" x 42"; crosscut into a total of 24 squares, 2⅜" x 2⅜". Cut 8 squares once diagonally to make 16 half-square triangles.
- 1 strip, 7⅛" x 42"; crosscut into 4 squares, 7⅛" x 7⅛". Use remainder of strip to cut one 7" square.
- 1 square, 10⅝" x 10⅝"; cut twice diagonally to make 4 quarter-square triangles

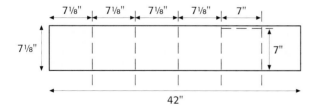

From the red print, cut:

- 1 strip, 2⅜" x 42"; crosscut into 16 squares, 2⅜" x 2⅜"
- 1 strip, 2" x 16"; crosscut into 8 squares, 2" x 2"
- 1 cardinal
- 3 strips, 2½" x 42"

From green print 1, cut:

- 4 squares, 2⅜" x 2⅜"
- 2 squares, 2¾" x 2¾"; cut each once diagonally to make 4 half-square triangles
- 10 holly leaves

From green print 2, cut:

- 8 of polygon template
- 8 holly leaves

From green print 3, cut:

- 10 holly leaves

From the dark red print, cut:

- 8 of diamond template

From the lengthwise grain of the floral print, cut:

- 4 strips, 3½" x length of the fabric

Assembling the Quilt Top

1. Draw a diagonal line on the wrong side of each 2⅜" tan square. Place one of these squares on top of a 2⅜" red square, right sides together. Sew ¼" from the drawn line on both sides. Cut on the drawn line. Press the seam toward the red. Repeat for remaining squares. Make 32.

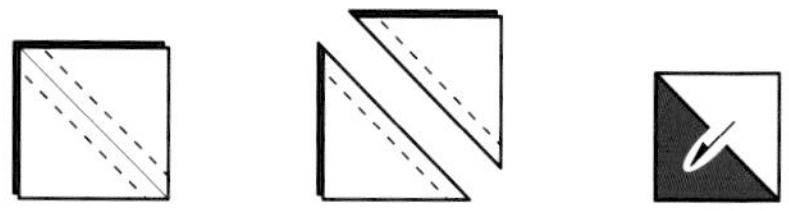

Make 32.

2. Draw a diagonal line on the wrong side of each 2⅜" green print square. Place one of these squares on a corner of the 7" tan print square, right sides together, as shown. Sew on the drawn line and trim seam to ¼". Press the seam toward the green print.

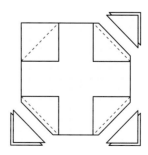 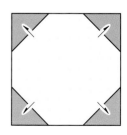

Make 1.

3. Join two half-square-triangle units, a 2⅜" tan print half-square triangle, and a dark red print diamond. Press. Make 4. Join a 2" red print square, two half-square-triangle units, a 2⅜" tan print half-square triangle, and a dark red print diamond. Press. Make 4.

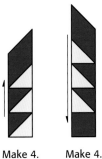

Make 4.   Make 4.

4. Sew units made in step 3 to the sides of a 7⅛" tan print square as shown. Press.

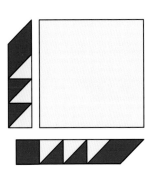

Make 4.

5. Join two half-square-triangle units and a 2⅜" tan print half-square triangle. Press. Make 4. Join a 2" red print square, two half-square-triangle units, and a 2⅜" tan print half-square triangle. Press. Make 4.

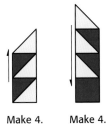

Make 4.   Make 4.

6. Sew units made in step 5 to a 10⅝" tan print quarter-square triangle. Sew the short unit to a short side of the triangle as shown. Start stitching at the edge of the large tan triangle and stop stitching 1" from the point of the pieced unit. Press the seam as shown, stopping at the end of stitching.

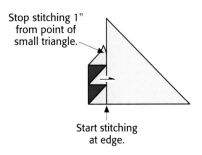

Stop stitching 1" from point of small triangle.

Start stitching at edge.

7. Sew the longer unit to the other short side of the triangle; start stitching at the edge and stop stitching 1" from the point of the pieced unit. You'll complete these seams after the units are joined to adjacent units. Press the seam as shown, stopping at the end of stitching.

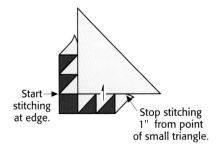

Start stitching at edge.

Stop stitching 1" from point of small triangle.

8. Sew a green print polygon to the side of the pieced triangle unit. Press.

9. Sew a 2¾" green print half-square triangle to a green print polygon and press. Sew this unit to the pieced triangle unit and press. Make 4.

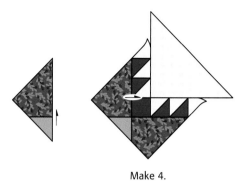

Make 4.

10. Arrange the star in three rows of three units as shown.

11. Sew the units in each row together. Stitch from the straight edge to the diagonal edge as shown, being careful not to catch the tips of the large tan triangles in the seams.

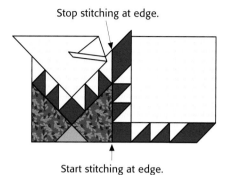

Stop stitching at edge.

Start stitching at edge.

Complete the seams, matching the raw edges as shown. Press.

Finish stitching seam.

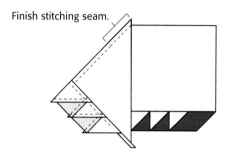

12. Sew the rows together, making sure to match the seams between the units. Press the final seams toward the center row.

Finishing

1. Using one of the appliqué methods described in "Basic Appliqué" on page 9, prepare the appliqué pieces.

2. Arrange the cardinal and the leaves as shown in the quilt plan below. Machine or hand appliqué as desired.

3. Machine or hand embroider the details on the cardinal: stitch the mask black, the beak yellow, and outline the wing with red thread as indicated on the template.

4. Attach the borders to the quilt top, following the directions in "Straight-Cut Borders" on page 13.

5. Stack the backing, batting, and quilt top and then quilt the layers, referring to "Quilting Techniques" on page 15 as needed.

6. Refer to "Finishing" on page 17 to bind and label your quilt.

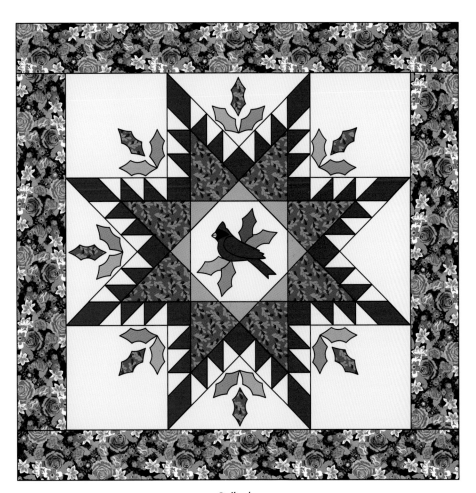

Quilt plan

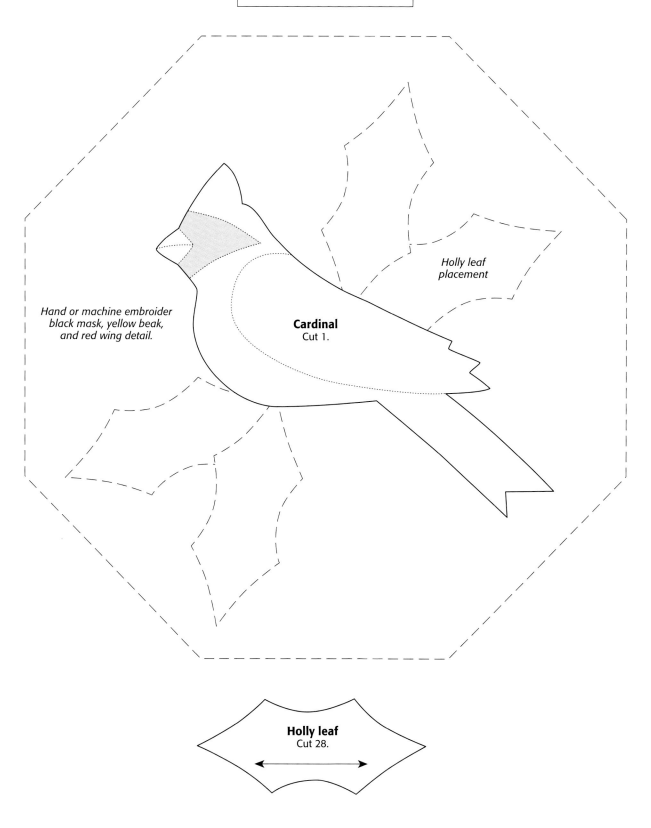

No seam allowance is needed
for fusible-web appliqué.
If desired, add ¼" seam allowance
for hand appliqué.

Holly leaf
placement

Hand or machine embroider
black mask, yellow beak,
and red wing detail.

Cardinal
Cut 1.

Holly leaf
Cut 28.

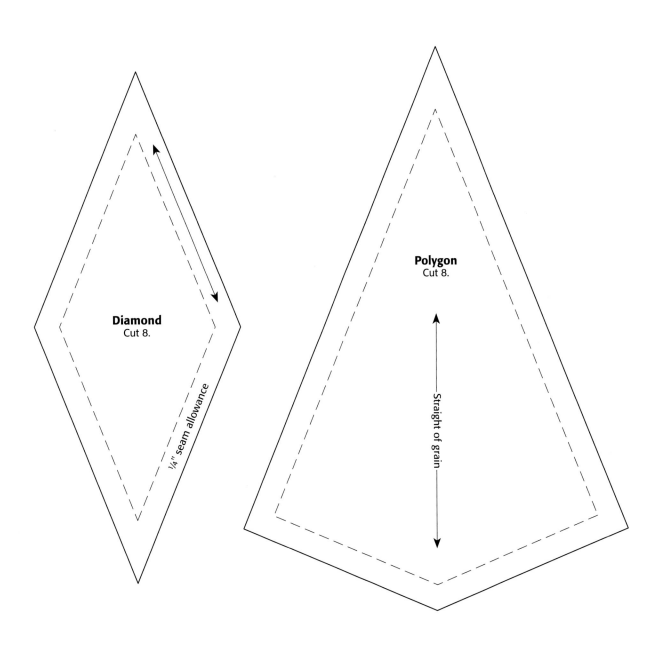

Diamond
Cut 8.

¼" seam allowance

Polygon
Cut 8.

Straight of grain

Brown Paper Presents

By Carol C. Porter, 1993, Everett, Washington, 65" x 65".

FINISHED BLOCK SIZE: 12" x 12"

Materials

Yardage is based on 42"-wide fabric.
- ★ 3¾ yards of green floral print for blocks, outer border, and binding
- ★ 2¾ yards of tan solid for blocks, setting triangles, and corner triangles
- ★ 1⅞ yards of green plaid for blocks and inner border
- ★ ⅜ yard of red vine print for blocks
- ★ ⅜ yard of red plaid for blocks
- ★ 4¼ yards of fabric for backing
- ★ 73" x 73" piece of batting

Cutting

All strips are cut across the width of the fabric unless indicated otherwise.

From the tan solid, cut:
- ★ 4 strips, 4½" x 42"; crosscut into 52 rectangles, 2½" x 4½"
- ★ 8 strips, 2⅞" x 42"; crosscut 4 strips into 52 squares, 2⅞" x 2⅞". Remaining strips will be used for strip sets.
- ★ 10 strips, 2½" x 42"; crosscut 6 strips into 16 rectangles, 2½" x 10½". Cut remaining strips into 60 squares, 2½" x 2½".
- ★ 2 squares, 12¼" x 12¼"; cut twice diagonally to make 8 quarter-square triangles
- ★ 2 squares, 9⅜" x 9⅜⅜"; cut once diagonally to make 4 half-square triangles

From the red vine print, cut:
- ★ 2 strips, 2⅞" x 42"; crosscut into 26 squares, 2⅞" x 2⅞"
- ★ 1 strip, 2½" x 42"; crosscut into 8 squares, 2½" x 2½"

From the red plaid, cut:
- ★ 2 strips, 2⅞" x 42"; crosscut into 26 squares, 2⅞" x 2⅞"
- ★ 1 strip, 2½" x 42"; crosscut into 8 squares, 2½" x 2½"

From the green floral, cut:
- ★ 4 strips, 6" x 72", from the lengthwise grain

From the remaining green floral, cut:
- ★ 14 strips, 2½" x 42"; crosscut 7 strips into 104 squares, 2½" x 2½". Remaining strips will be used for binding.
- ★ 4 strips, 4⅞" x 42"; crosscut into 26 squares, 4⅞" x 4⅞". Cut once diagonally to make 52 half-square triangles.

From the green plaid, cut:
- ★ 2 strips, 1½" x 42"

From the remaining green plaid, cut:
- ★ 4 strips, 2" x 60", from the lengthwise grain

From the remaining width of the green plaid, cut:
- ★ 13 rectangles, 1½" x 6¼"

Assembling the Blocks

1. Referring to "Adding Squares to Rectangles" on page 8, sew a 2½" green floral square to one end of a 2½" x 4½" tan rectangle. Trim both layers ¼" away from the seam. Press toward the green floral.

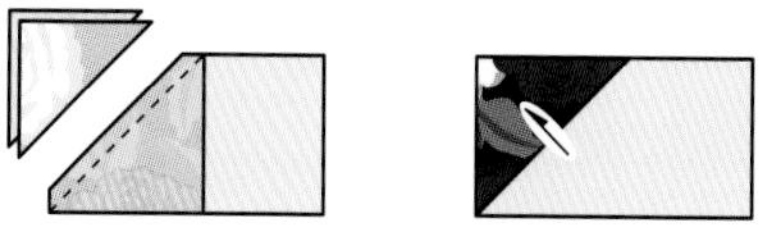

2. Place another 2½" green floral square on the opposite end of the tan rectangle. Sew, trim, and press as before. Make 52 units.

Make 52.

3. Draw a diagonal line on the wrong side of each 2⅞" tan square. Place one of those squares on top of a 2⅞" red plaid square, right sides together. Sew ¼" from the drawn line on both sides. Cut on the drawn line. Press the seam toward the red plaid. Repeat using the remaining red plaid squares. Make 52. Repeat using the 2⅞" red vine squares. Make 52.

Make 52.   Make 52.

4. Sew one 2⅞" tan strip to both sides of each 1½" green plaid strip. Press the seams toward the tan. Crosscut strip sets into 2⅞" segments. Make 26.

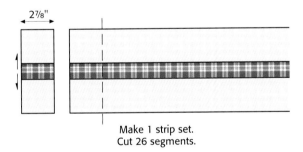

Make 1 strip set.
Cut 26 segments.

5. Sew a unit from step 4 to each side of a 1½" x 6¼" green plaid rectangle. Press toward the rectangle. Make 13.

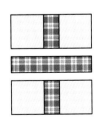 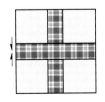

Make 13.

6. Make 13 blocks using the flying-geese units, half-square triangle units, 4⅞" green floral triangles, and 2½" tan squares. Press.

Make 13.

Assembling the Setting Triangles

1. Referring to "Adding Squares to Rectangles" on page 8, sew one 2½" red plaid square to one end of a 2½" x 10½" tan rectangle, right sides together. Trim the seam to ¼" and press toward the red plaid. Cut the opposite end of the rectangle at a 45° angle as shown. Make a total of eight plaid units, four oriented in one direction and four in the other, as shown. Then, using

the red vine print, make a total of eight units, orienting them as shown.

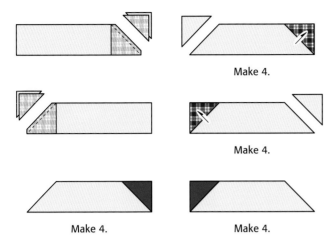

Make 4.

Make 4.

Make 4.   Make 4.

2. Assemble a setting triangle using units from step 1, a 12¼" tan quarter-square triangle, and a 2½" tan square. Press. Make four with the red plaid. Make four with the red vine print.

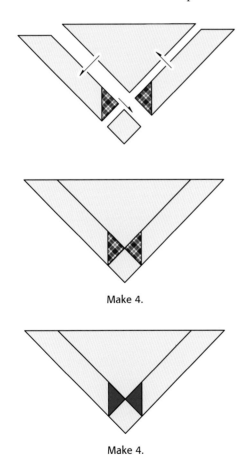

Make 4.

Make 4.

Assembling the Quilt Top and Finishing

1. Arrange the blocks and triangles as shown. Join the blocks in diagonal rows, pressing the seams in opposite directions from row to row. Join the rows, aligning the seams between the blocks. Add the corner triangles last. Press the triangle seams toward the corners.

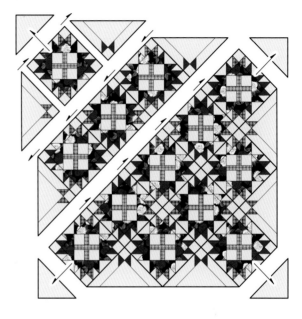

2. Mark the center of each border strip by folding it in half crosswise and pressing lightly. Sew each inner-border strip to an outer-border strip, matching the centers. Make four sets.

3. Add the borders to the quilt top, following the directions in "Borders with Mitered Corners" on page 14.

4. Stack the backing, batting, and quilt top and then quilt the layers, referring to "Quilting Techniques" on page 15 as needed.

5. Refer to "Finishing" on page 17 to bind and label your quilt.

Finding the Right Quilting Design

Quilting is the final detail that can enhance a quilt and bring it to it's full potential. Whether you decide to hand or machine quilt, a quilt like "Brown Paper Presents" offers great opportunities to showcase your quilting. The side and corner setting triangles of any diagonally set quilt are perfect places to use interesting quilting designs. In comparison with the rest of the quilt, they are fairly large areas with no seams to interfere with your stitching. The large diamonds that are formed where the blocks are sewn together are secondary areas for focus quilting. These areas can be enhanced by using a quilting design that is similar to that used in the outer setting triangles.

Choosing a quilting design for your border is generally determined by the value and pattern of the border fabric. To create visual balance within your quilt, try to use some curved designs within a pieced quilt to balance the straight lines and angles. If your quilt is primarily appliqué, using straight lines such as crosshatch quilting helps to balance the curves of the appliqué shapes.

Cranberry Wreath

By Retta Warehime, 1994, Kennewick, Washington, 65" x 83". Quilted by Vi McDonald, Spokane, Washington.

FINISHED BLOCK SIZE: 12" x 12"

Materials

Yardage is based on 42"-wide fabric.

- ★ 3¾ yards of tan for background and border
- ★ 2 yards of dark red (red 5) for blocks, sashing, inner border, and binding
- ★ 1 yard of dark red (red 3) for blocks
- ★ ⅝ yard of medium dark red (red 1) for blocks
- ★ ⅝ yard of dark red (red 2) for blocks
- ★ ½ yard of light red (red 4) for blocks
- ★ ½ yard of light red (red 6) for blocks
- ★ ⅛ yard of dark green for sashing squares
- ★ 5 yards of fabric for backing
- ★ 71" x 89" piece of batting

TIP: *Cut a small piece of each red fabric. Tape the swatches to an index card and number them for quick reference.*

Cutting

All strips are cut across the width of the fabric unless indicated otherwise.

| Fabric | FIRST CUT | | SECOND CUT | |
	No. of Strips	Strip Width	No. of Pieces	Dimensions
Tan	3	2⅜"	36	2⅜" x 2⅜"
	7	2"	144	2" x 2"
	7	3½"	144	2" x 3½"
	3	6½"	18	6½" x 6½"
Red 1	4	2"	72	2" x 2"
	2	3½"	36	2" x 3½"
Red 2	4	2"	72	2" x 2"
	2	3½"	36	2" x 3½"
Red 3	12	2"	216	2" x 2"
	3	2⅜"	36	2⅜" x 2⅜"
Red 4	4	3½"	72	2" x 3½"
Red 5	4	3½"	72	2" x 3½"
Red 6	4	3½"	72	2" x 3½"

Assembling the Units

To avoid confusion, group the units by number and label each group. After adding each piece to a unit, trim the excess fabric and press.

1. For unit 1, sew a 2" red 2 square to the left side of a 2" x 3½" tan rectangle as shown; trim both layers ¼" away from the seam. Press the seam toward the red piece. Sew a 2" red 3 square to the right side of the unit; trim. Press the seam toward the red piece. Make a total of 36 units.

Unit 1.
Make 36.

2. Refer to the diagram to sew, trim, and press units 2, 3, and 4. On unit 2, press the seams toward the red pieces; on units 3 and 4, press the seams toward the tan pieces. Make a total of 36 of each unit.

Unit 2.
Make 36.

Unit 3.
Make 36.

Unit 4.
Make 36.

3. For unit 5, sew a 2" x 3½" red 5 rectangle to the right side of a 2" x 3½" red 4 rectangle. Press the seam toward the red 4 piece. Sew a 2" x 3½" red 6 rectangle to the right side of the unit. Press the seam toward the red 4 piece. Add a 2" red 3 square to each end of the unit. Press the seams toward the red 3 pieces. Make a total of 72 units.

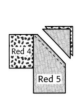
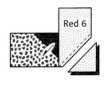

Unit 5.
Make 72.

4. For unit 6, draw a diagonal line from corner to corner on the wrong side of 36 of the tan 2⅜" squares. With right sides together, pair each marked square with a 2⅜" red 3 square. Sew ¼" on each side of the marked line; cut on the marked line. Press the seams toward the dark red pieces. Make a total of 72 units.

Unit 6.
Make 72.

Assembling the Rows

1. Row 1 and row 5 are identical. Using 2" tan squares, 2" x 3½" tan rectangles, and units 1 and 2, assemble 36 rows as shown. Press the seams toward the tan pieces.

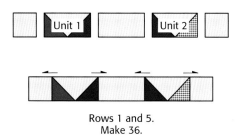

Rows 1 and 5.
Make 36.

2. Row 2 and row 4 are identical. Using units 3, 4, and 5, assemble 36 rows as shown. Press the seams toward units 3 and 4.

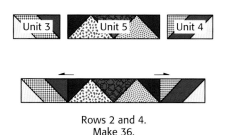

Rows 2 and 4.
Make 36.

3. Row 3 is used twice in each block. Using a 2" x 3½" tan rectangle and two of unit 6, assemble 36 rows as shown. Press the seams toward the tan rectangles.

Row 3.
Make 36.

Assembling the Blocks

1. Arrange the rows, two of unit 5, and a 6½" tan square as shown in the diagram. Sew the rows in the following order:

★ Sew row 1 to row 2. Press the seam toward row 1.

★ Sew row 4 to row 5. Press the seam toward row 5.

★ Sew row 3 to unit 5. Press the seam toward row 3; repeat for an additional unit. Sew these two units to opposite sides of the center square. Press the seams toward the square.

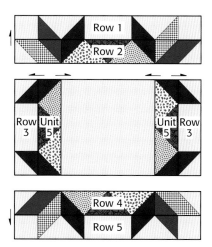

2. Sew the combined top and bottom rows to the center section to complete one Cranberry Wreath block. Press the seams toward the outer edges. Make a total of 18 blocks.

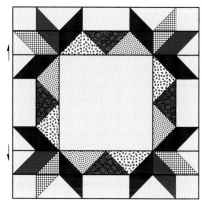

Make 18.

Assembling the Quilt Top

| Fabric | FIRST CUT | | SECOND CUT | |
	No. of Strips	Strip Width	No. of Pieces	Dimensions
Background				
Tan	2	19⅝"	3	19⅝" x 19⅝"
	1	10¾"	2	10¾" x 10¾"
Sashing				
Red 5	16	1½"	48	1½" x 12½"
Green	2	1½"	31	1½" x 1½"
Borders				
Tan	7	3½"		
Red 5	7	1½"		
Binding				
Red 5	8	2½"		

Adding the Sashing and Borders

When sewing the sashing to the blocks, be consistent in the orientation of each block, with rows 1 and 2 always at the top. It's also helpful to sew with the block on top of the sashing strip so that you can see the points.

1. Sew one 1½" x 12½" sashing strip to the right side of each block. Press the seam toward the sashing.

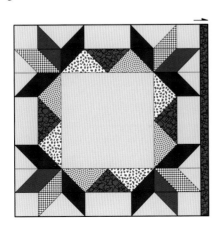

2. Sew additional sashing strips to the blocks as shown. Make two rows of three blocks, and two rows of five blocks. Press the seams toward the sashing.

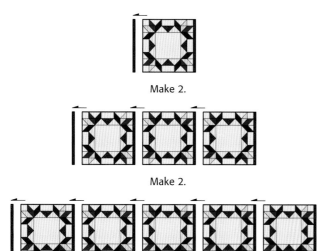

Make 2.

Make 2.

Make 2.

3. Refer to the diagram below to join the 1½" green sashing squares to the remaining 1½" x 12½" sashing strips. Make two rows with one sashing strip, two rows with three sashing strips, two rows with five sashing strips, and one row with six sashing strips. Press the seams toward the sashing.

4. Sew the sashing strips assembled in step 3 to the top of the rows as shown. Press the seams toward the sashing. Set aside the sashing strip made from six pieces.

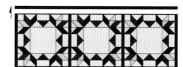

Rows 1 and 6.
Make 2.

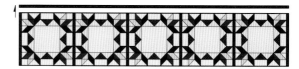

Rows 2 and 5.
Make 2.

Rows 3 and 4.
Make 2.

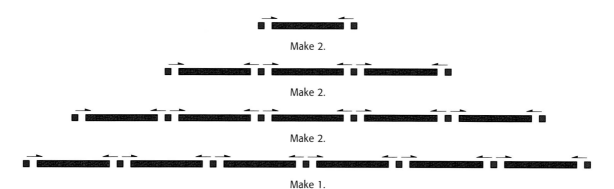

Make 2.

Make 2.

Make 2.

Make 1.

5. Cut the 19⅝" tan squares twice diagonally to make 12 side setting triangles. You'll use only 10. Cut the 10¾" tan squares once diagonally to make four corner setting triangles.

6. Arrange the rows, setting triangles, and remaining sashing strip as shown. Join the side setting triangles to the ends of the rows. Press the seams toward the triangles. Join rows 1 and 2, rows 3 and 4 (with the remaining sashing strip in between), and rows 5 and 6; join the sections. Press the seams toward the sashing. Add the corner setting triangles. Press the seams toward the triangles.

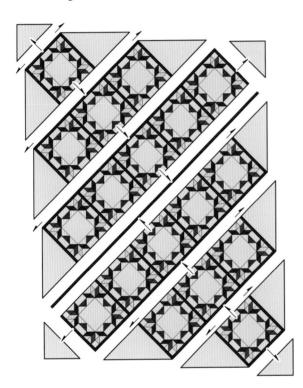

7. Add the inner border, and then the outer border, following the directions in "Straight-Cut Borders" on page 13.

Quilt plan

Finishing

1. Stack the backing, batting, and quilt top and then quilt the layers, referring to "Quilting Techniques" on page 15 as needed.

2. Refer to "Finishing" on page 17 to bind and label your quilt.

Crazy Heart Tree Skirt

By Iva Willard Galloway, 1992, Puyallup, Washington, 43" diameter.

Materials

Yardage is based on 42"-wide fabric.

* ★ 1 yard of red or green tone-on-tone fabric
* ★ ¼ yard *each* of 9 different Christmas prints
* ★ 2⅝ yards of fabric for backing
* ★ 2 yards of polyester fleece batting
* ★ ½ yard of fabric for bias piping (if making your own)
* ★ 10 yards of ⅛"-wide cording to make piping OR 10 yards of ready-made piping to coordinate with skirt fabrics
* ★ 2 Velcro dots or snaps
* ★ Gold or silver metallic thread
* ★ #8 perle cotton
* ★ Size 8 crewel needle
* ★ Assortment of laces, beads, ribbons, charms, and buttons

Cutting

The template patterns are on pages 79–80.

1. Trace the skirt center pattern from page 80 onto a piece of paper to make a template, marking the edges that will be placed on folds.

2. Cut a 36" x 42" piece of batting. Fold the fleece in half and then in half again. Place the skirt template on the folded batting as shown and cut it out.

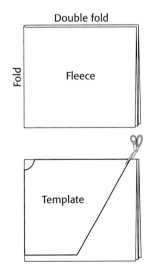

3. Using the tone-on-tone fabric and a 36" x 42" piece of backing fabric, follow the illustrations in step 2 at lower left to cut out the skirt center and the backing.

4. Unfold the fleece, the tone-on-tone fabric, and the backing fabric. Cut from the outer edge to the center of each piece on the straight of grain as shown. Adjust the size of the hole to fit your tree. The hole on the pattern fits most artificial trees.

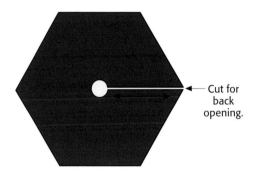

Cut for back opening.

5. Fold a piece of paper in half and make a paper template of the heart pattern. Cut six hearts from the remaining fleece as shown.

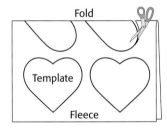

6. Cut six hearts from the remaining backing fabric. Set aside until Crazy-quilt piecing has been completed.

Assembling the Hearts and Piecing the Crazy Quilt

1. Using a permanent marker, mark fleece hearts as shown. Dividing the heart shape into sections (not necessarily equal) is an easy way to approach Crazy-quilt piecing. Divide the heart into two sections first.

Then divide one of the areas with another line.

2. Label the areas 1, 2, and 3 as shown below. Pieces are sewn into area 1 first, then into area 2, and finally into area 3. Pieces sewn in area 2 will cover the raw edges of pieces sewn in area 1, and pieces sewn in area 3 will cover the raw edges of pieces sewn in the other two areas. Mark arrows in each of the areas as shown. This indicates the direction in which the pieces will be sewn. Sew pieces in area 1 toward the V. Sew pieces in areas 2 and 3 parallel to the drawn line.

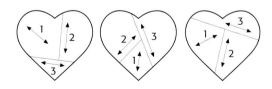

3. Cut pieces larger than they need to be to fit the desired space. Place the first piece of fabric right side up in area 1. Place a second piece of fabric,

right side down, on top of the first piece. Stitch a straight seam, ¼" from the edge. Flip the second piece open and finger-press.

Continue adding pieces in the same manner—sewing, flipping, and finger-pressing—until the area is filled. Don't sew only straight strips; angle some of your pieces to create rectangles and wedges. Just be sure you can cover the raw edges with the next piece.

4. Add pieces to area 2. Place the first piece right side down so that the right edge of the piece covers the raw edges of the pieces in area 1; stitch ¼" from the right edge. Flip the piece to the right side and finger-press. Add the remaining pieces until area 2 is covered. Alter the angle of the pieces to create interesting shapes.

First piece in area 2

5. Add pieces to area 3 in the same manner. Remember to cover the raw edges of the pieces in both areas 1 and 2.

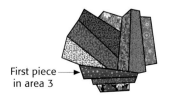

First piece in area 3

6. Trim the fabrics even with the fleece edges.

Adding the Piping

1. If you purchased ready-made piping, skip to step 4. If you're making your own, cut 1"-wide bias strips from your piping fabric. Join the strips at a 45° angle as shown to make one continuous strip, 10 yards long. Press the seams open.

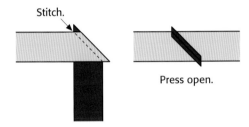

Stitch.

Press open.

2. On the wrong side of the bias strip, place cording down the middle. Fold the raw edges together, keeping the cording pushed against the fold. Attach a zipper foot to your sewing machine and position the needle in the left notch of the foot. Use long basting stitches (six stitches per inch) to sew the two raw edges together, enclosing the cording.

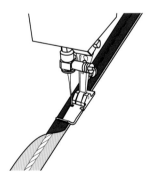

3. When the entire length of piping is sewn, trim the seam allowance to ¼" from the stitching.

4. Keep the zipper foot on the machine to sew the piping to the hearts. Place a pin in the middle of the V, ¼" from the inside point.

¼"

Align the raw edges of the piping with the raw edges of the heart. Leaving a 1" tail, begin sewing the piping where the pin was inserted at the V of the heart; backstitch. Don't stretch the piping as you sew around a curve; sew it evenly to the edges of the heart.

Start stitching at point of V, leaving a 1" tail.

5. Clip the piping seam allowance when you reach the point of the heart. Stitch to the corner. Stop with the needle in the fabric and lift the presser foot. Turn the fabric slightly and take two stitches across the corner. Lift the presser foot again and turn the fabric to sew the next side.

6. When you reach the starting point, stitch to within ½" of the V of the heart; backstitch. Trim the piping, leaving a 1" tail. Clip the V of the heart to the stitching line.

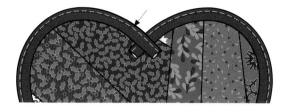

Stop stitching ½" from V of heart.

The beginning and end tails of the piping should overlap as shown. This will leave room to turn the piping to the wrong side when stitching the backing to the front.

7. Embellish the hearts with fancy embroidery stitches and beads if desired. Use a variety of colored or metallic threads for your embroidery. Below are some examples of popular embroidery stitches.

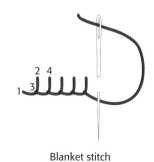

Blanket stitch

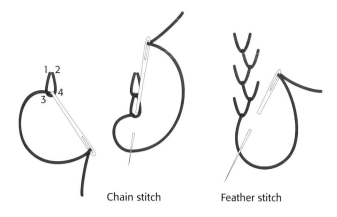

Chain stitch   Feather stitch

French knot

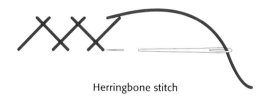

Herringbone stitch

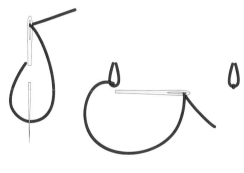

Lazy daisy stitch

Stem stitch

8. With right sides together, stitch the heart front and backing together, using ¼"-wide seams. Stop and start stitching ¼" from the inside corner. Leave a 4" to 5" opening on one side for turning.

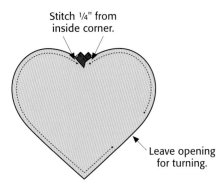

Stitch ¼" from
inside corner.

Leave opening
for turning.

Turn right sides out. The opening will be closed when the heart is stitched to the skirt center.

Finishing

1. Mark the quilting lines on the right side of the skirt center as shown on the skirt pattern.

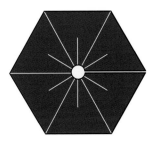

2. To make the tab closures for the skirt, cut two 3" squares from skirt-center fabric. Fold in half diagonally, then in half again.

3. Pin the folded triangles on one side of the opening, one near the center and one halfway down the side as shown.

4. Layer the skirt-center top and the skirt-center backing with right sides together. Place the fleece against the wrong side of the skirt-center top, matching the raw edges. Using a ¼"-wide seam allowance, stitch all the way around the outer edge, the back opening, and the center as shown. Leave a 5" to 6" opening on one side of the back opening for turning.

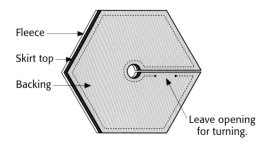

Fleece
Skirt top
Backing

Leave opening
for turning.

5. Turn right sides out. Smooth the layers out flat and machine quilt on the marked lines. Use a fancy stitch or fancy threads if desired.

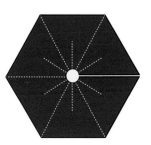

6. Place a heart on each section of the skirt center as shown. The sides of the hearts should meet at the outer edge of the skirt center. Using the zipper foot on your machine, stitch in the ditch between the piping and the heart top from one side of the heart around the point to the other side. Backstitch at both ends to secure stitching.

7. Sew Velcro or snaps to the tabs and tree skirt, to keep the skirt closed.

8. Make a label for your tree skirt.

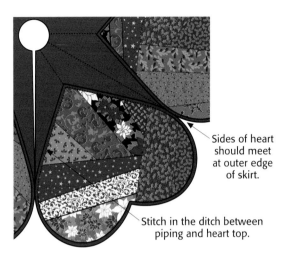

Sides of heart should meet at outer edge of skirt.

Stitch in the ditch between piping and heart top.

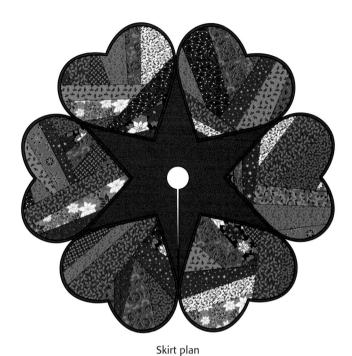

Skirt plan

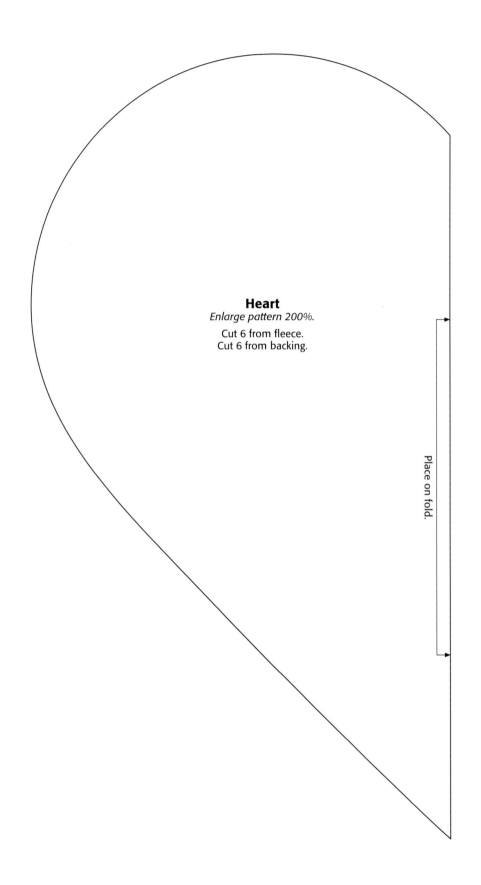

Heart
Enlarge pattern 200%.

Cut 6 from fleece.
Cut 6 from backing.

Place on fold.

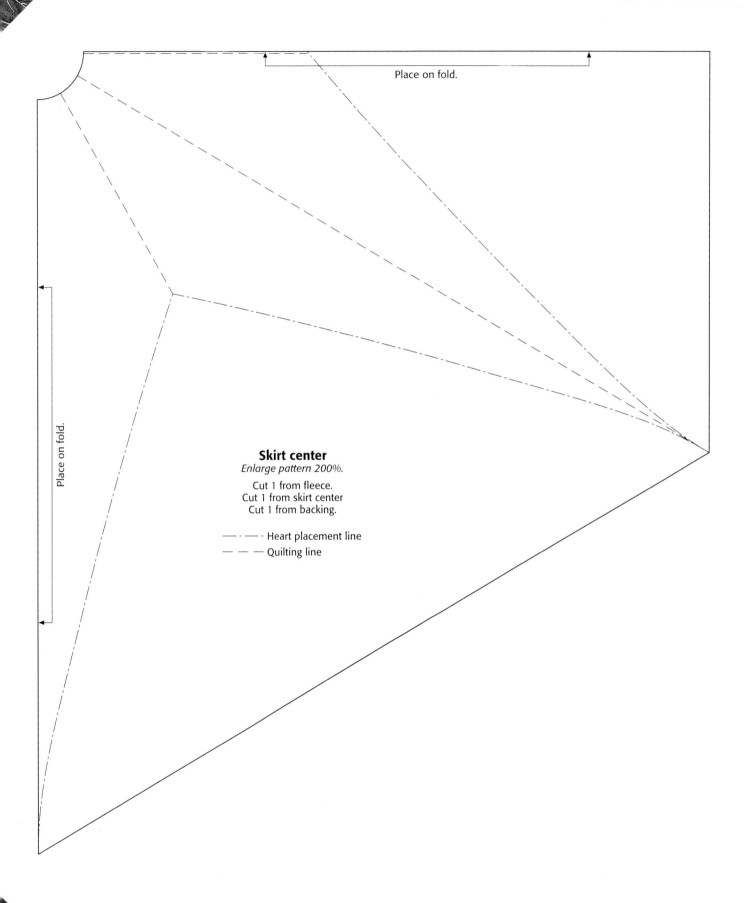

Place on fold.

Place on fold.

Skirt center
Enlarge pattern 200%.

Cut 1 from fleece.
Cut 1 from skirt center
Cut 1 from backing.

— ∙ — ∙ — Heart placement line
— — — Quilting line